CHRISTOPHER ISHERWOOD

By ALAN WILDE

Temple University

 173

Twayne Publishers, Inc.　::　New York

Twayne's United States Authors Series

Sylvia E. Bowman, *Editor*

INDIANA UNIVERSITY

Christopher Isherwood

For

JACK UNDANK

Preface

A T ONE point in *The World in the Evening*, Christopher Isherwood's protagonist, Stephen Monk, returns for the first time in over thirty years to his family home. Recalling his childhood habit of looking through a stained-glass window and "experiencing the pure pleasure of sensations which need no analysis," he goes on to contemplate, nostalgically and with some bitterness, his present mode of perceiving the world: "The whole organ of cognition had changed," he remarks, "and I had nothing left to know with. If I looked through the window now, I should see nothing but a lot of adjectives" (26). The romantic epistemology that underlies the comment—in particular, the sense of an unbridgeable gap between the child's world of unified perception and the fragmented awareness of the adult's—is specially prominent in *The World in the Evening;* but the more general psychological implications of Stephen's state of mind make him a typical figure among Isherwood's leading characters, almost all of whom experience, if not a feeling of separation from some earlier and better self, at least one of division between self and world.

In fact, it is the themes of separateness and aloneness—along with the repeated images of mirrors, games, and traveling (to mention only the most prominent)—that provide continuity among Isherwood's works. The works differ from one another, on the other hand, in the ways the characters respond to their dissatisfactions with themselves and the worlds of which they find themselves so remotely and unsatisfactorily a part. Here again Stephen provides a relevant example, illustrating as he does in the earlier stages of his life that penchant for escaping into fantasy or anger which characterizes the protagonists of Isherwood's early novels and, in his last phase, the movement (shared by those of the postwar fictions) toward the discovery of the "Atman," or real self, whose freedom from the constricting consciousness and self-consciousness of the ego promises the unity of all being.

What is true of Stephen's development is true of Isherwood's as well. It may be thought that the parceling-out of any artist's career into discrete and manageable segments reflects as much the critic's subjective need for order as it does the objective phenomenon of growth and change in the life of a particular writer. But in Isherwood's career it seems safe to say that the notion of two distinct periods is demonstrably true as well as critically convenient. Isherwood's departure for the United States in 1939, his espousal of pacifism, and his subsequent conversion to Vedanta mark a turning point in his career, which is no less dramatic for his continued concern with the self and, one may say, given the frequently autobiographical basis of his books, with himself. More to the point now is the fact that, with Isherwood's movement toward a newer country and an older religion, there comes a radical change in his critical reputation. Some of the reasons for this change are explicable enough. Isherwood produced, after all, only two novels during the 1940's and 1950's (however great the volume of his nonfictional writing), and these were, it is clear, generally of a quality inferior to what had preceded them. Furthermore, one must take into account the reaction against the inflation of Isherwood's reputation in the 1930's, the resentment at his leaving England with W. H. Auden shortly before the war, and the suspicions about his turn to religion. But the major reason for the devaluation of Isherwood's books, especially his novels, seems to lie above all in a failure to understand the nature of his vision.

To put the matter simply, it has become increasingly common among critics to assume the identity of Isherwood with his protagonists, especially with those of the first-person novels, and to assume further that he is, as the narrator of *Goodbye to Berlin* apparently claims to be, a neutral observer of the agitated scene that surrounds him. Beginning from this point, those who dislike Isherwood's work profess to find him trivial or morally insensitive; whereas those who seek to praise him, do so, no less destructively perhaps, for his elegance and humor. It has seemed to me most important, therefore, in the light of popular conceptions and misconceptions, to stress, even while trying to provide a comprehensive overview of Isherwood's career, the moral impulse that is to be found everywhere in his works.

The complexity and at times the ambiguity of that moral intention requires in turn a detailed study of technique. Critics who tend to misread the novels are generally guilty of missing at least part of their irony: specifically, the irony that is almost invariably directed at the narrators and protagonists of the books. Consequently, I have chosen to concentrate on the nature of and the changes in Isherwood's ironic consciousness over the past forty years and, in addition, in order to make clear the shape of his development, on the principal, though again changing, qualities of his style.

There is probably no living writer less justly valued at the present time than Christopher Isherwood, none, therefore, more in need of revaluation. The lack of any book-length study and the relative scarcity of articles devoted to his work testify to the state of general neglect. What has been accepted is Isherwood's importance to the literary history of the 1930's; what has still to be recognized is that, both before and since the war, he has been one of the period's most original ironists and one of its most subtle moral thinkers as well.

Acknowledgments

I should like to thank Professor Charles Burkhart for his kindness and patience in offering technical advice; Mrs. Sylvia S. Cobrin and Mrs. Philip Kimbel for their counsel and encouragement in my discussions of parts of the book with them; Mr. Robert Jackson for locating in England some material relating to Isherwood not available in the United States; Mr. Steven Goldstein for his conscientious work as my research assistant; Professor Sylvia Bowman for her careful reading of the manuscript and for her corrections; and Mrs. Michael Shapiro for typing the manuscript. Temple University has been most generous in awarding me several summer grants and a Research Study Leave, which enabled me to complete this book.

I am particularly grateful to Mr. Christopher Isherwood for his interest and for permitting me to question him during a long interview (from which I have, with his permission, quoted) about his work; to Miss Margaret A. Moan, who has been much more than helpful in aiding in the preparation of the chronology and bibliography of this study and generally as patient and generous in giving of her time as she has been astute in her comments and suggestions; and to Professor Jack Undank, who has read and criticized the whole of the manuscript carefully and with a concern for which I am very much in his debt.

For permission to quote from the works of Christopher Isherwood and from the plays and travel book written in collaboration with W. H. Auden thanks are due to Mr. Isherwood, to Mr. Auden, and to the following publishers: New Directions and Jonathan Cape (*All the Conspirators*); New Directions and The Hogarth Press Ltd. (*The Memorial, The Berlin Stories,* and *Lions and Shadows*); Random House and Methuen & Co. Ltd. (*Prater Violet* and *The World in the Evening*); Simon and Schuster and Methuen & Co. Ltd. (*Down There on a Visit, A Single Man, A Meeting by the River,* and *Exhumations*); Random House and Faber and Faber Ltd. (*The Dog Beneath the Skin, The Ascent of F 6, On the Frontier,* and *Journey to a War*); the Vedanta Press (*An Approach to Vedanta*).

Acknowledgments

For permission to quote from W. H. Auden's *Letters from Iceland, The Collected Poetry of W. H. Auden, Poems, On This Island (Look, Stranger!)*, and *Nones* thanks are due to Mr. Auden, to Random House, and to Faber and Faber Ltd.

I wish, finally, to acknowledge *Modern Fiction Studies* and the Purdue Research Foundation for permission to reprint, in somewhat altered form, the chapter on *Lions and Shadows*.

Contents

Chronology

1904	Christopher William Bradshaw Isherwood born August 26, in High Lane, Cheshire, England; son of Captain (later Lieutenant-Colonel) Francis B. and Kathleen Machell-Smith Isherwood.
1914–1918	Attends St. Edmund's School, Hindhead, Surrey, where he meets W. H. Auden. Father killed in action, 1915.
1919–1922	Attends Repton School where friendship with Edward Upward begins.
1923–1925	Attends Corpus Christi College, Cambridge on scholarship. Leaves Cambridge without a degree after deliberately failing examinations. In 1923, he begins work on a novel, *Lions and Shadows*, a book finished but never published.
1925	Secretary to Mangeot family in London.
1926–1927	Private tutor in London. Anonymous poem, "Souvenir des Vacances," appears in *Oxford Poetry*, edited by Auden and C. Day Lewis.
1928–1929	Medical student at King's College, London.
1928	Publication of Isherwood's first novel, *All the Conspirators*, by Jonathan Cape.
1929	Joins Auden in Berlin.
1930	Publication of his translation of Baudelaire's *Journaux Intimes*.
1930–1933	Teacher of English in Berlin.
1932	Publication of *The Memorial*.
1933	Leaves Berlin; spends summer in Greece. During the winter of 1933–34, he works on the screenplay of his first film, *Little Friend*, directed by Berthold Viertel.
1934–1936	Reviews for *The Listener*. From 1934–37 he lives in various European countries, returning to England for visits only.
1935	Publication of *Mr. Norris Changes Trains*; collaborates with Auden on first play, *The Dog Beneath the Skin*

1937	First performance of the second Auden-Isherwood play, *The Ascent of F 6*, in February. Publishes "Some Notes on Auden's Early Poetry" for the "Auden Double Number" of *New Verse* in November.
1938	Publication of *Lions and Shadows*, his autobiography. Leaves with Auden for China in January. Returns to England in July and works with Auden on last play, *On the Frontier*.
1939	Leaves with Auden for permanent residence in the United States in January. Meets Gerald Heard and Aldous Huxley, who introduce him to Swami Prabhavananda; becomes pacifist and Vedantist. Publication of *Journey to a War*, a travel book about China written with Auden, and of *Goodbye to Berlin*, his fourth novel.
1940	Works for Metro-Goldwyn-Mayer in Hollywood.
1941–1942	Works at American Friends Service Committee hostel for refugees at Haverford, Pennsylvania. Returns to Hollywood and collaborates with Swami Prabhavananda on a translation of the *Bhagavad-Gita*.
1943–1945	Editor of Vedantist magazine, *Vedanta and the West*.
1944	Translation of *Bhagavad-Gita* published.
1945	Publication of *Prater Violet*. Works for Warner Brothers.
1946	Becomes citizen of the United States.
1947–1948	Travels in South America and returns to England for first of several visits. Publications in 1947: translation with Swami Prabhavananda of *Shankara's Crest-Jewel of Discrimination*, revised translation of *Journaux Intimes*, first American edition of *Lions and Shadows* by New Directions. Works for Metro-Goldwyn-Mayer.
1949	Elected member of the United States National Institute of Arts and Letters. Publication of second travel book, *The Condor and the Cows*, about South America.
1950–1951	Writes seven reviews for *Tomorrow*.
1951	First performance in New York of John van Druten's play *I Am a Camera*, adapted from *Goodbye to Berlin*.
1953	Publication of *How to Know God: The Yoga Aphorisms of Patanjali*, translated with Swami Prabhavananda.
1954	Publication of *The World in the Evening*.
1958	Publication of *All the Conspirators* for the first time in the United States by New Directions.

Chronology

PART I *THE OLD GANG*

CHAPTER *1*

The Suburb of Dissent

L IONS AND SHADOWS is the most unpretentious exhibit in the vast gallery of Romantic and post-Romantic works that chart the development of the artist as a young man. Isherwood's preface invites the reader to treat the book as if it were a novel, but it is clear that, even where the work is untrue to fact, it is faithful to the inner struggles it exposes. Because of this and because it reveals in a form least affected by the requirements of fiction Isherwood's typical themes and concerns and his characteristic manner of expression, *Lions and Shadows*, although it is his fourth book, provides the best introduction to all of the novels and miscellaneous writings until the time of his decision to leave England for the United States.

In his note to the reader, Isherwood announces his theme with the statement that "this book is about the problems of a would-be writer"; he then adds: "The style is the man" (7).[1] The two statements are not completely coordinate: the first takes into account both the protagonist and the narrator and the nature of the development from one to the other; the second refers to information that can be inferred about the author-narrator alone. The latter, however, although less immediately obvious, is ultimately the more central figure in the book: at first sight simply bland, neutral, and cool, the familiar detached and impartial spectator of modern literature, the narrator supplies—in his observation and evaluation of the "education in the twenties" that transforms his younger self into the more sophisticated, thirty-three-year-old author of the 1930's—not only the angle of vision but also the moral values that the reader adopts in his interpretation of *Lions and Shadows*. The clue to his own personality and to that of the "implied authors"[2] of all the early novels lies, as Isherwood's epigrammatic sentence indicates, in the style or, more broadly, in the technique of the work—in the shaping voice that is everywhere, if lightly, felt as the major presence of the book.

I   The Style of Irony

Isherwood's handling of language has always been his hallmark, and critics have commented frequently on the ease and lucidity of his writing. Probably the most extended discussion of his stylistic technique appears in Cyril Connolly's *Enemies of Promise*, in which Isherwood appears as one of the chief representatives of the colloquial or "new vernacular" style.[3] Connolly is appreciative of and generally accurate about Isherwood's virtues, but to the degree that he sees him as part of a larger movement, in which Hemingway and Orwell figure most prominently, he is insufficiently aware of the variety and subtlety of his particular talent. None of the charges leveled at the practitioners of the colloquial style—"breathlessness," "the agitated dullness of the sentence," the "impoverished realist vocabulary"—applies in any meaningful way to Isherwood; and to speak of his "fatal readability" is, while paying a somewhat backhanded compliment, to miss much of the irony implicit in his prose.

It may be admitted, to begin with, that "purple passages" or "literary" effects are rare in Isherwood's writing. Certainly, his diction is simple; but what needs to be added is that the words are frequently deployed in such a way as to produce in the reader a sense of incongruity that is as potent as but less obtrusive and less blatantly grotesque than what one takes away from the early novels of Aldous Huxley, in which comparable strategies are employed. The result, in any case, is reductive: the reader is made to apprehend the texture of daily life as somewhat ludicrous, uncomfortable, even repellent.

Most descriptions in Isherwood's work are, in fact, written from an angle that is oblique to ordinary perception. Not only the ordering and arrangement but also the choice of words serves to bring about a slight but constant displacement of the reader's expectations, and it is Isherwood's accomplishment that even the most apparently random word or phrase contrives to fantasticate the entire passage of which it is a part. An example will demonstrate his characteristic method:

From the obelisk, you could see the whole sweep of the island coast away beyond Blackgang, to the southern headland, with the waves creaming in over the great red deserted beaches; seeming, at this distance, to be frozen to the shore in scribbled overlapping margins of dazzling foam. Far out, the sea was a dull violet haze. There was a strong peppery smell from the gorse and the sheep droppings on the sunburnt turf. Below, on the hot cliff face, the gulls circled and squawked; one, in particular, seemed to utter a kind of mirthless laugh. (235–36)

The progression in the paragraph—from what is, for Isherwood, an unusually rich and poetic description to the prosaically rendered comment on the gull; from "the waves creaming" to the equally vivid but more quotidian image of the foam, qualified as it is by the commonplace suggestions of the word "scribbled"; from that to the still more earthy and increasingly unpleasant suggestions of the smell, the droppings, and finally the squawking bird; from the kinetic and expansive opening view to the almost static desolation of the close—the whole progression is such as to diminish, to force the eye in a centripetal movement toward a joyless and all but empty center.

Lions and Shadows has its moments of exuberance, if not quite of intensity, and it is on certain levels at least a very funny book; but its persistent mode is deflation, its instrument the self-inflicted and barely noticeable pinprick. Diction, however, plays only a part, perhaps the smaller part, in creating the distinctive tone of the book; more elusively and, from the reader's point of view, less consciously, syntax gives shape to the author's vision. It is generally assumed that Isherwood's sentences are as simple as his vocabulary. Many are, and a typical one tends to organize a single impression, thereby imparting to the style of the book an effect of dryness and spareness and providing a formal equivalent to the discontinuities of perception that characterize the narrator's mind.

On the other hand, the ear, even sooner than the eye, will convince the reader that in almost any paragraph of *Lions and Shadows* there is to be found a number of long and complicated, and more rarely, of complex sentences. Of course, neither length nor complication is at variance with a style that is colloquial and familiar. Isherwood's sentences are never formally rhetorical or architectonic; the mind that they reflect is one in process, thinking discursively, as if in the midst of conversation, adding to, qualifying, or making more vivid some initial statement or observation, as in the following description:

In the great hall of the college, where many of our lectures were held, I could hardly keep my attention down to the subject for thirty seconds at a time; away it drifted, idly, like a child's balloon, around the ring of bent studious faces, then rising, to the enormous windows, to the Holbein over the dais, to the portraits of former Masters and dead notables—a salmon-pink, sneering Orpen, a suave tailored Sargent, a de Laszlo, a Watts—then higher still, to the carved beams and rich-coloured shadows of the famous sixteenth-century roof. (62)

Grammatically "compound-complex," the sentence, extended though it is, is not complex in any more ordinary sense of the word. Structurally imitating its content, it wanders and meanders; its short clauses accrete substance by the addition of a succession of still smaller participial, prepositional, and appositive phrases and of a number of adverbs and adjectives. Apparently as idly as the roaming attention it describes, the sentence orders itself by a process of casual addition, each of its members easily and informally deriving from the previous one and leading to the next; and each is sufficiently varied in size, organization, or grammatical form to disrupt any potential balance among them. The frequent commas mark the discreteness of the parts; the semicolon, of which Isherwood is almost as inordinately fond as Virginia Woolf, and the dashes make separation still more emphatic; so that one remains as aware of the identity of the individual and contributory elements as of the mosaic into which they are gradually formed. As in the passage previously quoted, the movement is from solidity to fragment, a movement of attenuation from the main props of the sentence to the increasingly distant and isolated members, from (to translate form back into content) the great hall to the shadowy reaches of the roof.

One more point needs to be made about Isherwood's style, specifically about the impact of an entire paragraph. Here it is not a question of diction or syntax but of the variety among and the concatenation of the sentences that compose the larger structural unit. The principle, however, is roughly the same: one is conscious of, or at least made to feel, a constant shifting among the kinds of sentences, a slight detachment of each from the others, a tendency to produce an effect of decrescendo toward the end. Everything follows, but nothing is explicitly related; an invisible hiatus fills the space after every period, producing for the reader the time needed to adjust to the minute but constant shifts of direction he is expected to make. Connectives, implicit or explicit, are rare in Isherwood's early prose; one is forced to jump, so to speak, rather than glide from one stop to another.

It would be naïve, of course, to pretend to a reading of a paragraph so pure as to ignore, in a discussion of the relations among sentences, the simultaneous pressures of those other aspects of style that have already been noted. In what follows, the interworkings of a number of different techniques are apparent:

Seven months later, on August 3rd, 1922, I woke up on board a cross channel steamer from Southampton, to find that Le Havre was already in sight. It was my first unforgettable view of anywhere abroad. The boat stole in towards the land across a flat grey sea, spreading heavy whitish ripples, as if through milk. The coast rose solemn behind the town. The tall houses were like shabby wings of stage scenery which had been left out of doors all night, propped against the cliffs. As we approached the quay, we heard the faint vigorous shouting of the inhabitants, the crowing of cocks and the clanging of the bells of trams. Bolsters were hung out from the windows to air in the pale sunshine. It seemed to me that the people here got up very early. (25)

The strategy of the paragraph is gradually to undermine the mildly romantic suggestiveness of the first two sentences (one is, as it seems, about to witness the young adolescent's first encounter with the foreign and the mysterious) by the introduction into the passage of elements increasingly incongruous with the expectations these raise. Not that the process is uniform and linear: just as the sentences vary throughout in length and grammatical complexity, so there is a jarring verbal alternation between the more picturesque and the more prosaic. In fact, the opening sentences themselves establish a pattern of syntactical and tonal asymmetry, and in the second a covert irony is created by the juxtaposition of the positive "my first unforgettable view" with the purposefully vague and flat phrase, "of anywhere abroad."

In its growing circumstantiality, the passage renders more and more ludicrous the reader's—and the protagonist's—anticipations of at least a minor epiphany. The image of the "flat grey sea," already somewhat disappointing, is made less appealing still in the participial phrase that qualifies it, and then is subverted completely by the mundane simile that follows. The next, short sentence, with its quasi-archaic dignity ("solemn" instead of "solemnly"), reawakens and reinforces for a moment the reader's initial impressions, which are then definitively overturned by the elaborate simile in the fifth sentence, in which the permanent and grand give way to the transient, the shabby, and the artificial. The sixth sentence supplements the disappointment of the eye with an assault on the ear, moving from the "faint vigorous shouting" to the discordant crowing and clanging. From this point, the climax of the paragraph, the movement is again downward toward a dying fall: after the feeble, idyllic echo of the penultimate sentence, there is in the last a total expiration, the triumph, brought about by the colorless diction and the insipid phrasing, of total inanition.

A number of different factors, then, work together to produce the sense of disparity and frustration that the passage engenders;

and tone, to the degree that it is not simply the result of style, also has its place. As Isherwood, or, rather, his friend Allen Chalmers, whom he is quoting, interprets it, tone is a matter of narrative as well as of stylistic technique: "We ought to aim at being essentially comic writers. . . . The whole of Forster's technique is based on the tea-table: instead of trying to screw all his scenes up to the highest possible pitch, he tones them down until they sound like mother's-meeting gossip. . . . In fact, there's actually *less* emphasis laid on the big scenes than on the unimportant ones. . . . It's the completely new kind of accentuation" (173–74). In the passage quoted about the arrival at Le Havre, it is clear that Isherwood is aiming precisely at the de-emphasis of the potentially important and exciting. Not only the language but also the selectiveness of the eye whose movement it records is at issue here: what the narrator chooses to see or not see, the events and incidents he does or does not set down, these too serve to define the quality of his imagination. Among the myriad of details he might have noted, the disillusioned traveler fastens on those that substantiate his inherent skepticism and prove to him that all places are much the same.

Style and the narrative technique that duplicates in another area its essential features; the tone that they combine to produce, with its perpetual slight mockery and denigration, its understatement and "tea-tabling"; and, as we shall see, point of view—all help to translate and, in turn, point to a vision of the world that can best be described as ironic. Irony in this context is not to be understood simply as an isolable literary technique. For modern man, it is a characteristic sensibility, a response—like sentimentality in the eighteenth and nineteenth centuries—to a growing loss of faith both in the reality of the external world and in the authenticity of the self. Both sentimentality and irony are attempts to cope with what Dickens called "the prison of this lower world," a world made mediocre by its exaltation of the average, dense by its accumulation of things, and frightening by its failure to make the material subserve the spiritual. Sentimentality's tactic is to assault the prison with a flood of warmth and intimacy, to try—with the benevolence of Sterne's Uncle Toby or the self-effacing altruism of Dickens's heroines—to melt away the obstacles of an unfeeling society, to establish a moist and tearful communion of emotion among human beings fallen prey to Gradgrindism and Podsnappery.

Irony, as it derives from the German Romantics and subsequent theoreticians, is, as compared with sentimentality, a later and more disillusioned response;[4] it aims not to transcend but to armor itself against the world. Less hopeful of achieving involvement with life or even of making sense of it, it provides a defense against hope; its perspective is one of distance and coolness; and, in place of the unguarded openness of emotion, it adopts the tentative and wary strategies of reason. Approaching life with the expectation of disappointment, irony anticipates the unexpected, stresses the gaps rather than the continuities of life, and precludes tragedy with disenchanted awareness. Its spirit can be found in the atonalities of modern music, in that conception, which dominates modern literature, of time as a collection of rare and precious moments rising out of the grayness of daily life, and in the presentation through the art of montage of the discrete particulars of experience assembled to make apparent the incongruities of an absurd world. Its country is that of Eliot's "Hollow Men," where the shadow falls "Between the motion/ And the act."

All irony demands the complicity of the reader and assumes a level of intelligence at least equal to the ironist's own. Isherwood's in particular calls for a degree of sustained attention without which even the most alert are likely to be betrayed into the mistaken belief that the apparently neutral and transparent narrator is simply the recorder, reporter, or, most famously, in *Goodbye to Berlin*, the camera that he purports to be. What is reflected by these various stances is, in the first instance, not methodology but psychology; not the supposedly bland empiricism of the scientist or the literary realist, but the involuntary detachment of the outsider. Whether or not he is being intentionally ironic, it is significant that the narrator of *Lions and Shadows* adds in apposition to his description of his younger self as "the would-be novelist" the phrase "the professional observer" (246). Isherwood's books take as their leading theme the failure of involvement and communication, the failure to establish contact between the self and the world. Viewed in this light, the seeming transparency is seen actually to be a mask and a shield: "Henceforward," the narrator says late in the book, "my problem is how to perfect a disguise" (248).

The difficulties of penetrating the perfected disguise are threefold. It has already been suggested that the narrator calls little *overt* attention to himself. The lightness of his touch and the refusal to dramatize himself make him the most unobtrusive of guides through what he calls "the vast freak museum of our neurotic generation" (217). Furthermore, there is a remarkable consistency in maintaining the tone of the book: "the wry, the sotto-voce,/ Ironic and monochrome," as Auden puts it in the

poem from which the title of this chapter is taken.[5] Irony is pervasive, not occasional; there are no excursions into sentimentality, as
in Forster's novels, or into anger, as in Huxley's. Few modern
writers exhibit in their works a more uniform texture or provide
fewer jolts to the reader's absorption in narrative surface. *Lions
and Shadows* is, in fact, a study in low relief: all of the characters,
incidents, and objects are viewed from the same distance and
with the same amount of interest. So in his opening note, Isherwood refers to the "caricatures" he has drawn; and, although he
is at that point indicating primarily the lack of correspondence
between his characters and their real-life models, there is some
validity in the remark: characterization is largely external; there is
little probing of minds, little effort to lay bare the inner life.

Isherwood's conception and articulation of his characters bear
little resemblance to the methods of the modern psychological
novel. Here, as elsewhere, his approach is oblique: the reader is
presented with surface and left to infer depth. The characters in
Lions and Shadows—and in all of the novels where the protagonist bears Isherwood's name—are less individuals in their own
right than facets of the protagonist and then of the narrator-
author. Everyone whom the young Isherwood meets throughout
the course of *Lions and Shadows* is in some way an objectification
of a quality, good or bad, that is inherent or potential in him; each
is what he might be, what he revolts against, or what he is. Necessarily, since the record of his thoughts and actions supplies the
narrative interest of the book and his development, its unifying
thread, the protagonist receives more attention, but the difference
is one of degree, not kind. Ultimately, he, like the others, is part
of the network of clues that refers back to the narrator who is
recording his education.

II   Evasions and Failures

Early in the book, as he prepares to leave his public school for
Cambridge, the young Isherwood tells Mr. Holmes, the actorlike
teacher who is the first of his models, that he wishes to be a
writer. The response comes in the form of "a lecture, half-mock-
ing, half-serious, on the value of drudgery, the need for breadth,
the necessity of getting inside the minds of people differently
constituted from myself" (47). Thus the primary theme of the
autobiography is announced: the need to transcend the limiting
boundaries of the ego and to establish some authentic relation not
only with other isolated individuals but with the world at large. It
is in these terms that one is to interpret the remark that Isher-

wood makes, when, in commenting that his book is about the problems of a would-be writer, he adds that, because it is, "it is also about conduct." Conduct refers to the ways in which the protagonist acts or frequently does not act in his encounters with a series of people and places in the 1920's, and, specifically, to what he must learn and overcome in the course of his education if he is to become an artist.

Lions and Shadows, then, is a study in limitation and, more ambiguously, in growth. Its irony is directed most consistently at those fundamental traits that lead to the deficiencies and subterfuges of the protagonist and especially at their successive manifestations: the aberrations of conduct which keep him at the borders and not at the center of life. The nature of his character and conflicts is articulated most fully by means of two recurrent symbols—Mortmere and The Test—which correspond to the evasions and the failures of the protagonist (hereafter, Christopher to distinguish him from Isherwood, the narrator-author). Mortmere, a bizarre village invented and peopled by Christopher and his friend Chalmers with a group of mad grotesques, is the concretion of all the vivid fantasies that provide an escape from the unsatisfactoriness of daily living. The Test—which is the burden of "the neurotic hero, The Truly Weak Man," who, as Isherwood describes him in *Lions and Shadows* and embodies him in the early novels, prefers to the "direct, reasonable route" that "The Truly Strong Man" follows "the laborious, terrible north-west passage, avoiding life" (207–8)—is the challenge, generally sublimated, invariably feared, of meeting the pressures of the everyday world.

Whereas Mortmere leads only to the construction of a private world and a private vocabulary, The Test, on occasion at least, precipitates Christopher into action, but his gestures are in fact as whimsical and unreal as his daydreams: there is, after all, little to choose between the elaborate conception of an eternal war waged by "The Rats' Hostel" or "The Other Town" against "The Enemy" and the decision (made when he finally volunteers for duty during the General Strike) to work on a sewage farm because it has "a sort of spurious Mortmere flavour" (180). Both symbols point to the protagonist's underlying fear, which in turn finds expression in two repeated images: the one expressive of his complete rejection of and revolt against the adult world; the other, of his retreat from it—the nursery and acting. "Charade," "stage," "theatre" (in addition to the already noted "mask" and "disguise"), "Nanny," and "nursery clock" all recur rhythmically in *Lions and Shadows* to define Christopher's self-consciousness and

immaturity and to create, in the light of his life-defeating attitudes, the irony of the book's title, taken, as the narrator explains,
from the phrase: "arrant lovers of living, mighty hunters of lions
or shadows . . . " (75).

If Mortmere, anarchic in content as it is in form fantastic, and
if The Test, derived as it is from "a complex of terrors and long-
ings connected with the idea 'War' " (75), reveal Christopher's
dislike and distrust of authority, they point still more obviously to
his essential loneliness and aloneness. More and more insistently
as the book goes on, the note of dissatisfaction is sounded: "I
wanted to stop playing the rebel myself. I wanted to be absorbed
in the crowd" (290). Not that Christopher is another in the long
line of alienated waifs and strays of nineteenth- and twentieth-
century fiction. Surrounded by a solicitous family, enjoying the
substantial benefits of his upper-middle-class background, he
moves easily through the social world of the college "Poshocracy"
and the artistic world of his friends, the Cheurets. The major
character contrast of Lions and Shadows is between Christopher
and his close friend Chalmers,[6] and its point is to show that the
former is, in his personal relations as in his writing, the more
facile, the more flexible, and the more successful in blocking
awareness of his problems. Less ironic and more intense, Chalmers moves from Mortmere, of which he is the originator, to communism; and he exposes by the seriousness of his concern the
compromises and the "more complex psychological mess" (120) of
the protagonist.

On the other hand, Christopher suffers, if less consistently or
dramatically, as intensely as his Romantic predecessors. "Lonely"
is another of the book's recurrent words, and its context generally
indicates the area of sexual failure. There are friendships, certainly, but these suggest, on the one hand, a search for self-defini-
tion and, on the other, a defensive alliance against the world at
large. In his enormous impressibility, Christopher, like a more
mundane Stephen Dedalus, easily and willingly identifies with
others. His imagination, however, draws not on figures from myth
and history but on his small circle of intimates: "I . . . reflected,"
the narrator says at one point, "that at least seventy-five per cent.
of my 'personality' consisted in bad imitations of my various
friends" (239). Throughout Lions and Shadows, one has glimpses
of Christopher creating order and romance in his life by seeing it
through borrowed eyes or, if he is left to his own resources, by
immediately transforming it into the subject for an anecdote; it is
the habit of all of Isherwood's early protagonists, the victory of the

artistic mind over prosaic matter in a battle not to face the exigencies of their own situations.

Taken as a whole, his friends, even the most aggressive and liberated, represent for Christopher a bulwark against the sea of general humanity. But the sense of being islanded, with or without his friends, in the midst of exactly those people who ought, he feels, to figure in his books grows on Christopher, as he discards one after another of his masks in disgust. What the process of stripping away reveals to the reader is the underlying egoism, the self-concern, that characterizes not only Christopher but also, with mounting intensity, the protagonists of each of Isherwood's novels. Egoism does not imply any necessary satisfaction with the self; indeed, in Christopher's case the reverse is true: discontent leads to self-absorption, and self-absorption in turn makes impossible any satisfactory relation to the outside world: the non-I pressing in upon the resentful and sensitive ego. In some ways, the two can be seen as the same or at least as mutually dependent: the sense of a self burdened by its own selfhood is articulated by a network of daily harassments, which are the objective forms of the inner dissatisfactions. Thus the alternating masochism and revolt and thus the constantly frustrated desire to escape: "You may give your familiar everyday self the slip easily enough," the narrator comments, and adds, "But, sooner or later ... that gloomy male nurse will catch you up; will arrive, on the slow train, to fetch you back to your nursery prison of minor obligations, duties, habits, ties" (269).

III   The Limits of Education

The ultimate desire, never consciously acknowledged and perhaps never fully understood in *Lions and Shadows,* is to lose the self, to destroy with one gesture personal identity and its reflection, the "nursery prison," the world as threat and punishment. In fact, the loss of the self, the abnegation of individual identity, is the goal toward which all of Isherwood's work strains; and *Lions and Shadows* is its most crucial formulation in the early period. It remains to be seen whether the book offers a solution, whether Christopher does in fact grow by the time he leaves England in 1929.

The final incidents of *Lions and Shadows* make the answers to these questions problematical at best. They involve, significantly, still another rejection and still another change of scene. The resolution to leave medical school is taken specifically in response to Hugh Weston's stories of Berlin and of the psychologist Homer

Lane, who via Weston and his disciple Barnard, offers the opportunity "to smash the nursery clock" and the "only hope of ever
growing up, at all" (307); but the description of Christopher's
movement toward the home of the new gospel (it is the last paragraph of the book) is so ambiguous as to make it difficult for the
reader to know how he is to respond: "Throughout the ten hours'
travelling which followed ... I thought, I suppose, of the future;
but ... I could see no farther than that evening, when I should
meet Weston, and, perhaps, Barnard himself. These two, between
them, would take care of everything. I was in their hands, and
content to be. One day, no doubt, I should start worrying again,
making plans and patterns, trying to organize my life. ... But for
the moment I was only a traveller ... happy in the mere knowledge that yet another stage of my journey had begun" (312).

One is reminded of Auden's distinction in "The Voyage" between the true journey and "the false journey [that is] really an
illness" (*Collected Poetry*, 168). The stress on Christopher's passivity, the conjunction of "plans" and "patterns," the recurrence of
the word "traveller"—all invite an ironic reading of the passage
and, with it, a judgment that nothing in fact has been solved and
that this decision, like most of the others made in the book, is
largely a negative one.

But it is difficult to be sure. The nature of Isherwood's irony is
to equivocate, to register the simultaneous awareness of different
possibilities without choosing among them. Like so many other
open-ended books of the twentieth century, *Lions and Shadows*
offers at its close a sense not of completion and certainty but of
speculation and doubt, posing most insistently the question of
whether there is any *substantive* difference between the Christopher of the late 1920's and Isherwood of the 1930's. The evidence
of technique indicates that there is not. At some risk of confusing
the differing requirements of and approaches to life and art, it is
possible to note the wide range of similarities between the ways
in which narrator and protagonist carry on their respective jobs of
writing and living: as Christopher continues to treat other human
beings and even his friends with a sometimes unwilling detachment, so Isherwood renders characters who are, by his own admission, caricatures; as Christopher passes through his education
relatively untouched by the experiences it has to offer him, refusing, if not growing awareness, then involvement and commitment,
so Isherwood takes the stance of the distant and disengaged observer; as Christopher conceives of his life as a series of fragments
and scenes, so the narrator adopts a narrative technique based

upon the presentation of discrete, and, except chronologically, discontinuous episodes.

Both Christopher and Isherwood are, in short, ironists, to use that term as I have defined it. "The goal of satire," Auden has recently written, "is reform, the goal of comedy acceptance."[7] One might add that the goal of irony is neither the one nor the other, but understanding. It may subserve the purposes of both, but its aim is, in modern literature and in its purest form, not a social but an individual one. The ironist strives, by emulating the distance and dispassionateness of God, the Romantics said, to liberate himself from the multiplicity and complexity of life, to neutralize, if not to overcome, the recalcitrance of the world and the self. In responding to an interviewer, who asked if he had any kind of reader in mind while writing, Isherwood answered in a way that is symptomatic and revealing: "No, I don't think so. One's friends, of course, to some extent. Yet more and more I write for myself, I think. More and more, writing is appearing to me as a kind of self-analysis."[8] Self-analysis is what, on one level at least, *Lions and Shadows* is, and it is also what Christopher achieves as a result of his education. Problems are posed, difficulties acknowledged, but of any significant change beyond the perfecting of a disguise there is no evidence.

To say that irony seeks understanding and liberation is not to deny that there is implicit in it a point of view toward the very things it wishes to rise above. The search is born out of precisely that vision described earlier: the sense of failure that is anterior to the undertaking, the disappointment that precedes the event. In this sense alone Christopher's orientation is less thoroughly ironic than Isherwood's: his thoughts, as he rides on the train at the end of *Lions and Shadows*, are, however indefinite, hopeful; it is Isherwood who qualifies, who casts doubt upon the future. But even this difference is a minor one; the traveler is on his way not only to Berlin but to *The Berlin Stories*, to a disillusion more settled and uniform but hardly more intense than what he already feels. What is at issue here is the characteristic state of mind; and that, in both cases, is wary, doubting, and disenchanted.

Disenchantment is, however, obviously no bar to creativity. The Christopher who leaves England is not merely on the threshold of his vocation; he is the author of *All the Conspirators* (1928) and of a first draft of *The Memorial* (1932)—almost half of what Isherwood himself had written by the time he completed *Lions and Shadows* (1938). What then of the point that is made repeatedly in the book from the preface onward—that good writing is contin-

gent upon the involvement of the writer with the people and in
the life of his times? Certainly the book shows, as Isherwood's
career does generally, that the life and writings of an artist are
interrelated, and *Lions and Shadows* has limitations, notably lack
of breadth and variety, comparable to those illustrated in the character of Christopher. But the fear that, "as long as I remained a
sham, my writing would be a sham, too" (305) proves to be beside
the point. On the contrary, the book demonstrates conclusively
that one need not solve his problems in order to write well; that
art may arise, if not from confusion, then from irresolution; that
the problematical is as fertile ground as the certain for the cultiva-
tion of an attitude toward the self and the world.

The final irony of *Lions and Shadows* is that its very existence
disproves its thesis. Style is the man and it is the artist too, and
conduct shapes all three—but to different ends. Isherwood's autobiography is a validation of itself rather than of the life it records, an ambiguous testimony to the triumph of the esthetic over
the moral. "Day after day," Stephen Spender writes about Isherwood in his own autobiography, "I witnessed that transformation
taking place in his mind, where the real becomes the malleable"⁹
and where, it might be added, the refractory is given satisfactory
definition in the timelessness of literature.

CHAPTER 2

Islands of Self

I The War Against the Old

ALL THE CONSPIRATORS is the angriest of Christopher Isherwood's novels, a gesture of defiance on the part of its younger characters and its author, a lively and sometimes incoherent attack on "the Family and its official representatives": "The Angry Young Man of my generation," Isherwood writes in his retrospective foreword to the first American edition of the book (1958), "called them hypocrites, he challenged the truth of what they taught. He declared that a Freudian revolution had taken place of which they were trying to remain unaware. . . . While they mouthed their platitudes, he exclaimed, we were all drifting toward mental disease, sex crime, alcoholism, suicide" (8). Whatever the final result of its campaign, *All the Conspirators* means to sound a cry to the barricades. The battle imagery is Isherwood's; the novel, he says, "records a minor engagement in what Shelley calls 'the great war between the old and young'" (8). Like "1929," Auden's poem about the need for and the possibility of regeneration, the novel demands, with total determination, if not with total conviction of success, "the destruction of error" and the "Death of the old gang" *(Collected Poetry,* 67).

The warfare, as Isherwood's remarks indicate, is psychological above all; and the chief enemy is Dorothy Lindsay, widow, matriarch, and survivor of a dead (or deadening) Edwardian world. Progenitor of that line of "Evil Mothers," as Cyril Connolly calls them,[1] who appear in Isherwood's work, Mrs. Lindsay symbolizes all that is worst in the Family. Surrounded by a vaguely threatening clutter of old-fashioned objects, she dominates her female household (in which the unfortunate and somewhat dubious exception is her son Philip) with a variety of methods—"treacle soaking through skeins of wool" (80) and "domestic guerilla warfare" (127) are two of Philip's descriptions—and with general success. Masking her strength under the appearance of weakness, using tears and sighs as her primary weapons, she is in everything

27

slippery and oblique: a master in the art of inspiring not fear but guilt.

The official representatives of the family, Mrs. Lindsay's coadjutors in the business of repressing the young, are made to seem, depending upon whether they are active or passive in their support of the old order, either menacing or absurd. The former especially suggest Isherwood's description of the effect on him of hearing Rudyard Kipling read at his own school: "I was terrified by Kipling's warnings—if Life was as rough as he made it seem, I knew I would never be able to cope with it—but that wasn't the only effect it had on me. I also became aware that the things he approved of—the Empire, the Flag, the Old School Tie and the Stiff Upper Lip—were various aspects of an Enemy whom I personally would have to fight, whether I liked it or not, for the rest of my life."[2] *All the Conspirators* is the first and, as has been suggested, the most overt stage of that fight in which the Enemy appears in all its guises and in which Isherwood's responses, apart from being transferred directly to his younger characters, are made manifest through his technique: together, point of view and characterization establish for the reader an external perspective from which he views the adult world—the conspirators against youth to whom the book's title appropriately, if not intentionally, refers[3]—in the simple and distorting light of the author's rage.

The victims of the old gang are treated very differently. Empathetic and ironic by turns, Isherwood's narrator, who enters freely into the minds and feelings of the younger characters, invites the reader now to observe them with distance, now to participate in "a James Joyce thought stream" (9), as Isherwood calls their interior monologues and reminiscences. The reader, consequently, is made both more aware of the greater complexity and individuality of the four young people who are the book's major interest and more sympathetic to their attitudes and problems. With their inner lives exposed, it becomes clear that all four share certain fears and exhibit certain, usually negative, responses in their attempts to cope with their ludicrous and repressive elders and with the world they have made.

Like the speaker of Auden's "1929," Allen, Philip, Joan, and, to a lesser degree, her more conventional fiancé, Victor Page, suffer the "restlessness of intercepted growth" (64) which manifests itself as acute boredom and physical nausea. Allen in particular, the most self-aware and romantic of the four, feels from time to time "helpless and physically sick" (15), but all of them experience the oppression of empty lives. Understandably, they respond to this emptiness either by escaping into fantasy and imagination or—in a more significant, because a more profound, reaction to their state of suppression—by exploding into violence. Instances of such outbreaks in the book are frequent and often comic: like minor Raskolnikovs, generally incapable of action but anxious nonetheless to assert their identities against the ennui of the average and the ordinary, they act, when they do, precipitously and many times destructively. And Philip's life, as the most inhibited, is appropriately the most violent in texture; compounded of sudden decisions and sudden attempts at escape, it is the most thorough and least successful effort to overstep the psychological barriers of the self.

None of the characters, in fact, are able to establish the link between self and world, and their mingled sense of desire and failure is made most apparent in their inordinate self-consciousness. A network of often repeated words—"smile," "grin," "watch," "blush," "flush," and "eyes" are the most common— suggests both an acute awareness of an outside world that is hostile or frightening and, even more, a sense of oneself as an object of others' consciousness. All, predictably, are most defensive and most embarrassed when sexually challenged or sexually aroused: having been made to feel inadequate by repression experienced at the hands of parents and schoolmasters, and made violent by their sense of inadequacy, they fear sex even more than they desire it. Therefore, when sexuality is acknowledged in their world, it is generally connected (by them *or* by the narrator, who again betrays his likeness to his characters) with what is ludicrous, morbid, or disgusting: Allen's boredom is "like hunger or love" (15); and, as he and Philip look at a group of rocks, they see, or perhaps the narrator sees, a medley of fantasy ("the winged horse and the gorgon, molars or fists of giants ... "); sexuality ("thigh, torso, buttocks, limbs, phallic symbols male and female"); and— now the perception is Philip's alone—death ("three corpses, and the centre one has got its stomach eaten out by rats") (19–20).

Against this ambivalent background, the sexual failures and the panic of the young people are revealed throughout the book. Philip, who is made queasy by the sensual atmosphere of the summer streets and particularly by the "increased sexual vitality" (124) of the girls he passes, is, as usual, the most devious in the acknowledgment of his emotions, the most successful in disguising them. His dream of sexual incompetence, in which he sits, terrified, in a train without an engine while a group of people waits and watches him, gives the problem its extreme form. It is treated most extensively, however, in the relationship of Joan and Victor.

As a matching of the most and the least liberated, the engagement of Joan and Victor predicts the inevitability of conflict or, at
the least, uneasy compromise. Victor, as Isherwood suggests in
Lions and Shadows, where the young man is called "a Cambridge
Poshocrat-athlete" (174) and where he is, much more obviously
than in *All the Conspirators,* cast in the role of villain, follows in
the line of Forster's Wilcoxes—symbols of the inadequacy of the
outer life and of the inability to connect. Eager though inarticulate
in the chase, he becomes, once engaged, totally embarrassed by
any talk of love; and Joan, in one moment of clairvoyance, sees
what her married life will be like (her thoughts are rendered by
some generalizing voice of, it seems, the older generation): "When
I am asked what good the War has done us, I say this: That it has
brought about a cleaner, saner relationship between the sexes.
The young people of to-day, with their short-cut hair and simple
healthy clothing are a whole world away from the days of Oscar
collars and hobble-skirts. ... Nowadays, there is no concealment,
for the excellent reason that there is nothing to hide" (183–84).

Joan's vision is the central comment on the crippling effects of
the older generation on the sexual lives of the young. It is also a
comment on the nature of interpersonal relations in general. Told
that they ought to have nothing to hide, the young people have
a sense, more or less acknowledged, of hidden depths which they
are at pains to conceal. Thus one finds the ironic situation in
which each feels he is transparent to all the others, whereas there
is in fact minimal communication among them. And because each,
guilty, fearful, unhappy, is so self-concerned, the self becomes a
prison, in which all four, individually, lead their isolated lives,
helpless against the unspoken accord of their elders.

II   The Genuine Forms of Life

The essential separateness of the characters is symbolically indicated from the beginning in the island setting of the first three
chapters, reminiscent of those islands which in the mythology of
the late 1920's and 1930's frequently suggest escape, isolation,
and psychological immaturity.[4] "This is an island and therefore
/Unreal," Auden writes in a poem addressed to Isherwood;[5] and,
against the landscapes and seascapes of the Scilly Isles, Allen,
Victor, and Philip begin to expose the unreality of their lives. The
problem is set with Philip's claim that he has "an enthusiasm for
... more *genuine* forms of life" (18) and is enlarged in the narrator's description of the Western Rocks (he is following Allen's

and Philip's gaze out to sea) as "clumsy smooth shapes of protean aspect, at different angles, to different eyes" (19). There is, in other words, a question of value and one of vision. Both questions are developed—the former, in Philip's attempt to define the word interesting; the latter, in a series of references to points of view— during a number of querulous conversations between the two boys.

The phrase, the "genuine forms of life," comes, in the context of the novel as a whole, to suggest the need for that involvement, most specifically interpersonal and sexual, of which the young people are so conspicuously incapable. The discussions that Philip and Allen hold help to define the relative incapacity of each and to show, in Auden's words again, that they and Victor are "Islands of self" who have "lost the way to action . . . " (*Collected Poetry*, 115). The concern with points of view refers not, as in so many twentieth-century novels, to the problem of relativism, but to the result of the inevitable failure of communication among the self-concerned. Allen at least shows an awareness of what the genuine forms are, but the "craving for the bizarre" (18) and the "purely literary point of view" (17) of which Philip, more perceptive about his friend than about himself, rightly accuses Allen, signify the latter's powerlessness to react spontaneously to those forms. "My callousness is diseased" (88–89), Allen tells himself, with the over-emphatic and self-punishing expressiveness that characterizes his thoughts about himself; and, more equably, he recognizes his habit of "taking attitudes towards things in advance" (94)—of protecting himself from the threatening incalculability of life. Intelligent enough to recognize that Philip, in his definition of the interesting as the ordinary, hardly knows what he means by the word, Allen is at least sensitive enough to suspect his own romantic and defensive postures.

Victor's is a simpler case. Lacking both Allen's sensitivity and his understanding, he reveals in the early chapters the uneasy blend of self-consciousness, priggishness, and superficial heartiness that later in the novel determines the course of his relationship with Joan. His entry into the argument as an example of the ordinary man is most important for allowing Allen to undercut Philip's philosophizing about the virtues of the ordinary—"He'd look at it," Allen says of the rock they have been discussing, "and say that it was a rock. A big rock" (21)—and for exposing through a particular example Philip's general failure of perception.

The failure, in creating a disparity between what Philip believes and what he inadvertently reveals about himself, provides the book with its ironic protagonist and, in his progress, with its ironic structure. Among the young people, Allen takes the role of rebel; Joan, of victim; and Victor, of surrogate for the old gang. Philip, encompassing all these, as well as Allen's negativism, Victor's impercipience, and Joan's unconscious imitation of their mother, points up what is common to them all and to the generation they symbolize: the failure, more or less severe, to emerge from the battle against their elders with the prize of authentic selfhood. Like *Where Angels Fear to Tread, All the Conspirators* falls into the general category of the *Bildungsroman;* but, even more extremely than Forster's novel, it stands the tradition on its head: Forster's Philip Herriton achieves partial growth and undergoes some education; Isherwood's Philip neither learns nor develops. Instead, he retrogresses, with decreasing awareness and degenerating moral fiber, from an early gesture of activity to, at the last, a state of passive and ludicrous defeat.

From the first, Philip's understanding of himself is suspect. His assertion of independence by an escape to the island rather than by direct confrontation with his mother leads the reader to believe, quite rightly, that his revolt is partial and marked by fear. Indeed, Philip's bickering with Allen about ethical and epistemological matters suggests less the desire to attack or convince his friend than to emerge triumphant in the vicarious dialogue with his mother, for whom Allen is patently a psychological substitute. The reader is invited to view even more suspiciously the devotion to art that is Philip's rationale for throwing up his humdrum office job, since the discrepancy between his professed artistic ideals, his supposed attachment to the ordinary, and his more characteristic mode of perception is extreme. Philip is, in fact, repelled by the ordinary when he comes upon it; and, even more than Allen, he is inclined to adopt a point of view that is dramatic and outlandish. "A would-be painter and writer," as Isherwood calls him in *Lions and Shadows* (174), he is not an artist at all but an esthete, one of that large group of twentieth-century characters who try to make life manageable by seeing it in esthetic terms.[6]

With his sulky return to the office, Philip's reaction against his mother and his imitation of her simultaneously increase until the tendency to martyrdom and self-pity that he shares with her leads Philip to initiate a second cycle of defiance, escape, and capitulation—a cycle which serves as an ironic parody of the first. Trapped by his family's failure to respond adequately to this gesture of infantile spite, Philip shows a primitive resourcefulness in his last-minute flight, which does credit to the determination of

his ego to survive on any terms. In the self-induced siege of rheumatic fever that results from that flight, Philip's lifelong hypo-
chondria is justified and Mrs. Lindsay's lesson that in seeming
weakness there lies actual strength is terrifyingly confirmed.

The closing scenes of the novel, dramatizing Philip's final ac-
quiescence in the ways of his mother, climax the book's horror and
point the lesson succinctly stated in one of Auden's poems: "Yours
you say were parents to avoid, avoid then if you please / Do the
reverse on all occasion till you catch the same disease."[7] That
Philip is totally unaware that he *is* sick, that in his recovery from
rheumatic fever he has given in to a more fatal disease, provides
the ironic perspective from which one views him—and his mother
—for the last time: Mrs. Lindsay, looking "years younger" and
"confidently gay" (240), thanks to the victory she has won and
which she is too wise to refer to or even to acknowledge to herself; Philip, his credentials as an artist certified by the sale of three
watercolors at a society bazaar and by second prize for one of his
poems in a newspaper contest, now the cynosure of the entire
household, waited on, petted, deferred to, a bewhiskered and be-
mittened child-man.

"You see, Allen," Philip tells his friend, sublimely oblivious that
what he is about to say he has said once before, "what I really
dislike about your attitude is that it gets you nowhere. You refuse
to venture, that's what it is. You're timid. Oh, I grant you one's got
to have the nerve ... " (255). The earlier occasion involves the
discussion of the genuine forms of life; the echo only underlines
what is now abundantly clear: that Philip's is in fact the least
genuine response to life in the book. He has traveled from the
island of self to, almost, the shores of madness, unaware that he
has made the journey.

The other characters fare only relatively better in breaking out
of their secondhand responses to life, although Allen's is the most
hopeful case. Philip finds Allen's messy room—he is the only un-
compulsive character in the book—"genuine of its kind" (132);
and, throughout the book, he seems the most clear-sighted both
about himself and about others. Indeed, he becomes more and
more the the measuring rod by which Philip is judged. But, like
Stewart Ansell in Forster's *The Longest Journey,* Allen can see the
truth without acting upon it or making contact with it. What one
is to make of him in the obscure "decrescendo of anti-climaxes"
(*Lions and Shadows,* 258) with which the book ends it is difficult
to say, or would be, if Isherwood had not indicated that, despite
Allen's apparently having overcome his feeling for Joan and found

a new love, he becomes "more and more proud, self-controlled, and Baudelairean."[8] "His battle cry," Isherwood says of his earlier self in his introduction to *All the Conspirators*, "is 'My Generation —right or wrong!' " (9). By the end of the novel there seems little question of which it is.

What then is one left with after the battle? A good deal of carnage certainly, the middle-aged spiritually dead, the young dying, and by implication a call to the reader for further action. Toward what goal it is not altogether easy to say, although *All the Conspirators*, of all Isherwood's novels up to World War II, attempts most unequivocally to give it a name. Thus, in the distance, never very distinctly defined, are the genuine forms of life, a suggestive equivalent to the "light" and "love" for which the 1930's poets, equally intent on the need for involvement, were in the habit of calling. Closer and clearer is the need to continue the work of destruction; in espousing this belief in the way that it does, the novel resembles most strongly the kind of committed and often tendentious writing that gave to the 1930's its most characteristic voice.

In tone and in imagery, *All the Conspirators* is at one with the poets who refer to "the lynx-eyed evil of the dying order"; who call for "Death to the killers, bringing light to life"; who announce that "It's now or never, the hour of the knife,/ The break with the past, the major operation"; and who ask: "How should I live then but as a kind of fungus,/ or else as one in strict training for desperate war?"[9] The urgency of the crusade is evident not only in the anger of the book but generally in the violence of its techniques. Isherwood himself has noted "a great deal of repressed aggression" (7) in the frequent obscurity of the novel; less expressive of repression are the structuring of the plot around a series of minor but explosive events, the abrupt shifts from consciousness to consciousness, the montagelike "cutting" from scene to scene, the staccato effect of much of the style, and the attempt to shock through absurd juxtapositions.

Nonetheless, one feels that, despite the immediate effect of violence that the book conveys, the action it demands is not in the first instance either the pursuit of the genuine or the crushing of the old gang—although these are desired as well—but rather the exploration of the self. Here, where Isherwood is at his most subtle and effective, where his touch is surest, one recognizes that he is also most vitally concerned. Indeed, in comparing authorial comments with those of the younger characters, one senses a coincidence of perception, tone, and quality of response that gives to the philosophical and psychological investigation a distinctly personal cast and reveals what the later novels make clear: that, ultimately, Isherwood's true subject is the self and most explicitly himself.

Indeed, from the start of his career, Isherwood contrives to combine morality with self-concern. The point is vital to the understanding of the novels that follow, and one of the chief values of *All the Conspirators* is that it helps to establish this insight. After 1928 Isherwood diverges, except in his plays, from the mainstream of 1930's writing, not because his books become so much more dependent upon the facts of his own life (the 1930's writers are almost obsessively concerned with themselves), but because increasingly they eschew anger and direct statement. Relying more and more on various kinds of indirection, the novels present in their description of the world of others what has often been taken for amoral reportage and, in their picture of their protagonists, what has even more frequently been taken as simple autobiography. They have been viewed, that is to say, as exercises in Naturalism and not as further forays into the battleground of the 1930's. The writers of the time, for whom Isherwood spoke with the voice of the generation, knew otherwise. Thus Auden in his birthday poem to Isherwood in 1935:

> So in this hour of crisis and dismay,
> What better than your strict and adult pen
> Can warn us from the colours and the consolations ...
> *Make action urgent and its nature clear?*[10]

Still the problem remains: what relation is there between the almost nagging self-concern of Isherwood (or Spender or Auden or Day Lewis) and his attempt to shape a better world? What exactly is the nature of Isherwood's commitment and of his moral position in general? An answer can be found in Michael Roberts's preface to *New Country* (1933), his important anthology of 1930's writers (including Isherwood). Speaking for those represented, he writes:

It is not easy for those who have once learned to question every thought and feeling to become again spontaneous, even when all the problems are solved—and they are not all solved yet. ...

That is why you will find us, in this book, satirising not only the enemy, but also our own past interests. For there are two kinds of satire: that which is directed at the known external enemy, and that which is intended to free us from our own preoccupations and indulgences so that we may stop the pitiful waste of thought and energy, which has made us as powerless and contemptible as we are.[11]

All the Conspirators employs both kinds of satire; but the second, with its suggestion of morality combined with therapy, is more congenial to Isherwood; and it defines the practice and aims of his increasingly autobiographically based novels. "We shall not perish" Edward Upward wrote as an epigraph to his novel, *Journey to the Border*, "because we are not afraid to speak of our weaknesses, and we shall learn how to overcome our weaknesses."[12] The sentiment is Isherwood's, although the tone accords only with his more tendentious first novel: there the battle is conducted on all fronts and openly; in the subsequent novels, warfare goes underground. In four years and in the atmosphere of Berlin, the angry young man becomes ironic.

CHAPTER 3

Exploring the Waste Land

T HE MEMORIAL, like Isherwood's first novel, is concerned with the attempt of the self to transcend its own subjectivity by managing both to assert its independence of the world of others and, on another level, to establish a connection with it: to achieve individuality while overcoming isolation. As in *All the Conspirators*, the concentration is on the goal of independence; but the greater complexity of *The Memorial* allows for additional consideration of what is to become the major concern of the immediately following novels: the necessity for involvement. Again, as in the earlier book, success is a question of choosing correctly between two opposed ways of life.

The contrast is made most explicitly by the book's protagonist, Eric Vernon, in an image that expresses the characteristic oscillation of his own mind as he considers his feelings for the village dominated by the Hall, home of the Vernons and, at the time, his own home, and for the village where his aunt and cousins are living:

Chapel Bridge and Gatesley were like the two poles of a magnet. Chapel Bridge—the blank asphalt and brick village, his village, clean, urban, dead —he called the negative pole. Gatesley—their village, lying so romantically in the narrow valley, its grey stone cottages surrounded by the sloping moors—that was the positive pole. And if you rode over from Chapel Bridge to Gatesley, from Gatesley back to Chapel Bridge, you were like a pin on a bit of metal filing, being drawn first by the one pole, then by the other. (173)

The formulation of negative and positive in terms of dead and romantic is Eric's, of course; and one of the lessons of *The Memorial* is that no character is to be relied upon absolutely in his perceptions of himself or of his world, but the tendency to render death concretely and life suggestively is also Isherwood's. In the novel as a whole, the choice is between, on the one hand, an allegiance to the dead forms of the past—the sheer weight of whose accumulated moral and physical debris works to crush and sap the vitality of the present—and, on the other, a liberation from them by means which are never made completely clear and toward a goal which remains tenuous at best, since none of the characters manages in fact to make a complete break with the past. It is, in other words, the opposition that in *All the Conspirators* is embodied in the "old gang" and the genuine forms of life, but that is here rendered far more variously and subtly and, in the case of the positive half of the polarity, more ambiguously as well.

I   The Dead

The symbols of death are particularly abundant, although some of them at least, in this novel of constantly deceptive appearances, suggest at first sight an ideal of openness, warmth, and gaiety. This is particularly true of the highly colored picture of Edwardian life that emerges from Lily Vernon's memories of her earliest visit to the Hall: "A beautiful, happy world, in which next summer would be the same, and the next and the next. ... The old safe, happy, beautiful world" (87–88). It is a familiar vision; to the reader attuned to the many primitivist novels of the twentieth century—*Howards End* is a notable example—there is no greater good than the life of stability and tradition: the sole hope of order in the chaos of the modern world. And the fact that Lily's perspective is that of the postwar world of 1920 only gives to her backward glance a greater poignancy, as it seems to give to the vanished Edwardian society even greater value.

But Isherwood in fact asks us to distrust Lily, or at least to recognize the relevance of her sentiments to her character, and to see behind the placid and elegant surface of life at the Hall snobbery, triviality, and emptiness: the complacent gestures of a moribund society epitomized in the inane and hearty Mr. Vernon and his sarcastic, selfish wife, who, to Lily, "make a most imposing royal couple" (87). Lily's regret assumes the destruction of value by unmerited catastrophe; Isherwood's irony implies a causal relation between the war and the way of life it partly brings to an end: the Vernons, along with the whole social and economic order they represent, are the first generation of the Dead.

The bitter fact *The Memorial* reveals is that the war changes nothing. To be sure, the more obvious relics of the Edwardian age do crumble and moulder, until they are, as it seems, hardly more than museum pieces. But if the war destroys the outward forms of life, it leaves untouched the centers of power. The monument that memorializes those who have been killed symbolizes in its rigidity and changelessness the past still impinging on the present and

inspiring in those who do not simply feel nostalgia for its authority
a sense of restlessness, guilt, and fear or, at best, of revolt. Bicy-
cling to Gatesley on the day of the dedication, Eric feels "the
strong negative pull of Chapel Bridge trying to drag him back-
wards like a harness. The Hall was behind it. His mother. All the
morning's scruples. The War Memorial itself" (174). What has
changed is the atmosphere: "The old safe, happy, beautiful
world," secure in its privileges and rights, gives way to the repressive, gray, self-conscious world that finds its chief embodiment in
the widowed Lily Vernon.

   The difference between *All the Conspirators* and *The Memorial*
is the difference between Isherwood's treatments of Mrs. Lindsay
and Lily. Lacking the clue of the author's anger, or any direct
authorial statement, the reader, who is invited to view Lily first
through the eyes of an admirer and permitted again and again to
enter into her thoughts and emotions, is likely to feel for her
initially a totally misleading sympathy. It is true that later in the
novel, as seen through Eric's eyes and in his thoughts, she reveals
increasingly her resemblance to Mrs. Lindsay; but in the context
of her situation and of Major Charlesworth's reverential attitude
toward her, she seems, as she imagines herself to be, the victim of
forces too mysterious to be understood and too wicked to be accepted. Like Forster's Ruth Wilcox, she appears in this perspective to embody the one hope, all the more noble for its futility, of
an England losing its sense of the past. But Isherwood is no
primitivist; and if the pity he invites for Lily reveals in part a new
understanding of the Enemy, an awareness that the destroyers are
to a degree at least themselves victims, still it is calculated much
more to make clear the subtlety of evil and to indicate the irony
of surface impressions.

   To this end, the descriptions of Lily are made from the start
highly ambiguous, so much so that perhaps only a second reading,
after the moral framework of the book as a whole has passed
judgment on her "reactionary romanticism" (9), reveals fully the
skillfulness of Isherwood's new technique. Her introduction into
the novel, by way of Ronald Charlesworth's mind, provides a good
example: "In appearance Mrs. Vernon was no more than thirty,
and yet a curiously mature air of sadness and quietness surrounded her, so that he knew, after a few moments, that she must
be ten or fifteen years older. She seemed sad, even though she
laughed and smiled and talked in a rapid eager way about old
pictures and old buildings. Since he had known her, she had been
dressed always in black, which accentuated the fairness of her

hair and skin and gave her sometimes absolutely the look of a child" (23).

The passage is filled with qualifications and with words that suggest an outward impression possibly at variance with some inner reality, and it is of course the awareness of several disparities in Lily's manner and mood that gives substance to Ronald's observations. But he is led, as a result of these, only to admiring acceptance of her—not surprisingly, since he shares her values so thoroughly. The reader, alerted by the equivocal manner of presentation, must recognize, however, something more disquieting in Lily; he must see in the particular paradoxes that are developed a paradigm of her inner life and values. Isherwood provides, with what henceforth becomes the main instrument of his understated and ironic rhetoric, a series of hints in the texture of the novel— somewhat akin to that varied repetition of words and phrases that Forster calls "rhythm."[1] Thus, most of the other characters notice, with a feeling very different from the Major's, Lily's strangely childlike quality, detecting in her an element of self-absorption and self-concern, which is underlined by her constantly looking into mirrors, by her diary, and by her strong awareness of herself as the object of others' concern.

This awareness accounts, much more than her actual grief, for the sadness that is again and again attributed to her and that provides another of the book's major rhythms. With an insistence that is apparent only when one has become aware of them, the words "sad," "silver," "silk," "smile," and "silent" are repeated in such a way as to surround Lily, when one of them is mentioned, with the sibilant alliterativeness of them all. So the faintly antique and precious associations of the silver and silk suggest Lily's worship of the past; the sadness and silence give to that worship an aura of mortuary calm; and the smile, most ambiguous of all expressions, sums up her ineffectual relations with the world of living people.

Isherwood's point is, of course, that Lily's childishness and her passion for anything and everything old are equally signs of death —the death of the spirit and of the heart. It is entirely characteristic of her that she eats "with the gestures of one who is never hungry" (45) and that her one activity after she leaves the Hall involves her membership in a Society, which weekly "visited some monument or relic of old London" (22). There she meets Ronald Charlesworth, and her relationship with him most obviously reveals her (and his) failure or unwillingness to find a connection with life, that is, with human beings, in the present. Again, the pattern of repeated images most effectively tells the story; throughout their relationship, Lily inspires Ronald with a reverential, sacred feeling: she is "a sort of nun" (25); her apartment is "as quiet and isolated as a shrine" (257); the silver teapot she hands to Ronald is "like a sacred vessel in a religious mystery" (255). Of course, it is not always easy to say whether the religious feeling is one that Ronald generates for himself or one that Lily inspires—he is several times described as a martyr, as when he is taking the elevator to Lily's apartment, "ascending into heaven" and making a "saintly gesture" (254). But the point probably is that both share the responsibility for paralyzing the relationship—for keeping it as sterile as the religion which sanctifies, in the Bishop's pompous oration, the memorial, the war, and the dead. In any case, Ronald's failure to propose, after Lily's disquisition on the Jacobean silver dish that was her wedding present, underlines her barren future and makes her the appropriate human embodiment of the book's "negative pole."

II   Rebels and Victims

All of the symbols of life, which are considerably fewer in number, cluster around Lily's sister-in-law, Mary Scriven, who in her actions and attitudes reveals a determination not to be borne down by the assumptions and demands of the past. Inspired in large part by a negative reaction to the Vernon way of life, she nonetheless achieves a degree of liberation to which no one else in the book attains. There is, therefore, a good deal of, if not entire, truth in her belief, as she looks backward over her life, that "she had done with the Past. The Past couldn't hurt her now" (287). Her vigorous association with music and art—meant to contrast with Lily's painting of pallid watercolors—and her haphazard love of crowds of people make her, whether in London or Gatesley, the center of a kind of creative mess, which leads her daughter to describe their house as "rather like the inside of a caravan" (12), the exact opposite of Lily's empty, lifeless flat. Constantly active, constantly organizing, Mary stands for the disordered order of change and movement, for what is happy, open, natural, and free. Standing in front of the Memorial Cross, she thinks: "All this cult of dead people is only snobbery. ... Living people are better than dead ones. And we've got to get on with life" (112–13). There is no question but that Isherwood agrees; at this point, at least, Mary speaks directly for her creator and perhaps for the 1930's in general.

But Isherwood hardly means to suggest that Mary is simply, in

Lawrentian or Forsterian fashion, the embodiment of the vital principle, or, more importantly, that such a principle is capable of full human realization in the world with which he is concerned. In other words, *The Memorial* superimposes on an ethical absolute a more equivocal vision of what is possible. As in one of Dickens's dark novels, there is a moral and psychological epidemic abroad which leaves no one unaffected. Mary is the closest one comes to a viable symbol of life, but the actual portrait of her is ambiguous, and there are aspects of her which seriously modify, if they do not quite cancel, our first impressions and make us realize that, as in his first novel, Isherwood can give concrete form far more easily to unmitigated evil than to absolute good.

Certain things about Mary immediately strike the wrong note, if one regards her as the ideal: the failure of her marriage, her resentment against men, the oversophistication that Eric notices, the ironic manner that both her daughter Anne and Lily comment upon, the air of contrivance about the almost chaotic freedom of her life. There is, one comes to feel, a quality of overreaction in Mary, which leads more easily to the subversion of Vernon ideals than to genuine involvement in life. Anne in particular, seeing her mother at closer range than the usually admiring Eric, notices with some irritation the artificially hectic tenor of life in the Mews —"Always this atmosphere of living in a railway station—just for the sake of living in a railway station" (12)—and, even more, Mary's humorous tolerance, which she comes close to recognizing as, but not calling, a somewhat cold-blooded indifference to others. Of course, Mary does feel a sort of diffused warmth for people and, provided that she is not forced to commit herself too far, a genuine interest in them. But she remains in the final analysis somewhat detached, the most vigorous actor in what she transforms into the game of life.

The metaphor is suggested by the recurrence of Mary's performance, apparently a frequent one, as Queen Victoria in a humorous charade. The choice of subject may or may not be significant (Victoria, chief representative of the "old gang," as the object of an ambivalent response, half imitation, half parody), but the action itself is certainly meant to symbolize the tendency to neutralize and contain life through humor. Edward Blake notices, early in Mary's married life when she is suffering under the disapproval of her parents, that she is "building up her fortifications" through a series of jokes intended to avoid "his tentative approaches and his unspoken sympathy" (138). And, at the end of the book, Isherwood underlines Mary's incompleteness by juxtaposing the scene in which she feels her liberation from the past with a final reference to the charade: " 'Very well,' said Mary, smiling. . . . 'But this is really and truly the very, very last performance on any stage.' 'Liar!' Maurice shouted" (288).

The actual choice that the other characters are presented with is, then, somewhat less clear than it at first seems. The negative pole is to be avoided; and, in fact, everyone in the second and third generation makes some effort, conscious or not, to escape from its influence, but the positive pole offers at best a direction, not a complete way of life. This direction the others attempt to follow; but, lacking Mary's vitality, their failures are all the more apparent. What they share is the tendency to create defensive surfaces against the rigors and disappointments of life, and so games—along with play, tricks, acting, and charades—become the leading metaphor, even more than in the case of Mary, for the quality of most of the lives in *The Memorial.*

Because the characters in the novel face a world even more oppressive, ominous, and threatening than the one in *All the Conspirators* (the opposition of Mary and Lily makes it obvious that the simple contrast of young and old no longer holds), their responses are correspondingly more exacerbated. The enormous self-consciousness and embarrassment that they feel (Anne looks into mirrors even more frequently than Lily) and their sense of isolation, of being outsiders, lead to the sensation of being surrounded, as Eric puts it, by "the proud enemies" (40). There is, as a consequence, a defensiveness in most of them that manifests itself, if not in the use of humor as a shield, then in the attempt to perfect disguises: Edward's sneer, Eric's "carefully and painfully prepared armour" (50), and the pretense of intimacy that Edward and Margaret project for the world are all examples. Occasionally, the mask slips; and, even when it has the desired effect on others, it does nothing to alleviate the internal awareness of separateness and alienation. So Eric feels, with an almost paranoid intensity, that "he must keep turning round and round lest some kind of area of danger should form behind his back" (39).

Walter Allen's comment that Isherwood's characters "are caught in an exquisite clarity of detail, yet, as it were, in isolation, somehow abstracted from the booming, buzzing hurly-burly of life"[2] is exactly right; as in *All the Conspirators,* they are cut off from each other by an extraordinary failure of communication that is illustrated more variously in *The Memorial* not only by the inability of anyone to understand anyone else but also by the constant narrative and stylistic conjunctions of scenes or phrases related only by what seems their accidental proximity. In the description of the crowd at one of Mary's concerts (35), for example, the abrupt transitions, the fragmented sentences, and the relative absence of ligatures provide the counterpart to the aimless fragments of unrelated chatter (obviously modeled on *The Waste Land*) and to the characters themselves, who are assembled for a discrete occasion and ready to disperse as soon as it is over.

What one has, then, in *The Memorial* is a world where essentially isolated people make frantic gestures of being in touch; where men and women, obsessed by a sense of inadequacy, are engaged in the Prufrockian business of preparing faces; and where it is impossible to fathom the depths by attending to the surfaces. And it is these disparities that make possible the pervasive irony of the book. Irony is, in fact, built into the narrative structure of *The Memorial*. The division of the novel into four nonconsecutive time blocks forces upon the reader the constant need to revaluate his first impressions and involves him, as fully as the characters themselves, in the difficult process of ascertaining the truth. Just as the apparently arbitrary juxtapositions of the individual scenes cause a sort of double take, so the juxtapositions of the larger units raise even more insistently questions of understanding and meaning. Along with a host of other twentieth-century novelists, Isherwood destroys linear time[3] in order to suggest the subjectiveness and fluidity of judgment in a world where the inner life is richer than the outer and where there is, thanks to the almost total breakdown of normative values, little congruence between reality and appearance.

Nothing makes clearer both how disparate the various possible views of a single individual or event are or how difficult are the comprehension and evaluation of one or the other than Isherwood's handling of a second technique: point of view. Identifying easily with character after character, entering impartially mind after mind, Isherwood's narrator is the first and perhaps most genuine of a line of cameralike recorders in his books. Refusing to commit himself beyond faithfully setting down what he sees without comment, he preserves an intransigent neutrality in the face of the confusing world he describes. The narrator, of course, is privileged to see a good deal more than any of the characters, but in other respects he closely resembles them. In other words, although his remarkably flat treatment of, say, the many deaths and accidents in the book or his incredibly easy passage from scene to scene and from character to character are the prime cause of the effect of understatement and "tea-tabling" throughout the book, it is hardly possible to credit him with intention because he is so totally devoid of normal consciousness and reaction.

It becomes necessary, therefore, to distinguish, as a number of critics fail to do,[4] between the narrator—whose irony suggests, like that of so many of the characters in *The Memorial,* a vision predicated on habitual disillusionment—and Isherwood, whose irony, whatever else it may represent, is the instrument of a conscious, satirical purpose, a sign of involvement, and not, like the narrator's, of distance and detachment. Isherwood's irony reveals the possibility of moral judgment; the narrator's assumes the indeterminacy of values. If, then, it is the narrator through whose eyes one first sees the images and symbols we have called "rhythms," it is Isherwood who is responsible for weaving these hints and clues into the texture of the work and who guides the reader in making his judgments after he has indicated, through the point of view, how hard these judgments are to make.

When the importance of the discrimination between Isherwood and his narrator has been granted, it becomes possible to ask whether there is not, after all, a resemblance between them: whether Isherwood does not display, at certain times and to some degree, a comparable tentativeness of approach that makes it difficult for the reader to be certain that he is possessed of all the direction necessary to proper evaluation of the characters and their actions. Anne's plan to marry Tommy Ramsbotham, possibly the most hopeful and affirmative event in the novel, provides the best illustration of the problem. Given the growth of Anne's feeling for Tommy, one is prepared, despite some blurring of the quality of and the reasons for that feeling, to accept the genuineness of the marriage and to find in the simple fact of connection and the promise of continuity a possibility of redemption in this sterile world. But the symbols that surround the marriage suggest another possibility. What significance is there in the fact that the wedding is to take place in Chapel Bridge, heretofore connected only with sterility, rigidity, and death? What in the fact that Anne and Tommy will eventually inherit the Hall, that decayed survivor of the past? What, finally, in the fact that Lily's gift is a Jacobean silver dish, given to her for her marriage and now passed ominously on to her niece? Are we to assume that Anne and Tommy will bring life back to Chapel Bridge, the Hall, the dish; that, within the context of their love, symbols are to lose their accustomed meanings?

It is asking a good deal of so small an incident as the wedding and of characters so minor as Anne and, particularly, Tommy; and, even if one adds that Anne is Mary's daughter and that power is therefore passing appropriately from Lily's family to hers, it is only fair to add that Mary's son Maurice gives every indication of being as barren as Lily's son Eric. Or is one to assume that Isherwood *means* to leave nothing untouched by his irony? In either case, the ambiguity remains, the difficulty of being certain that one's assumption is correct. Certainly there is here that rhetorical failure that Booth attributes to so much modern ironic writing—the failure to make clear to the reader how and to what he is to respond,[5] but there is also, one suspects, a failure of imagination, of a mind caught between faith and doubt and resolved in skepticism. Whether Isherwood intended to affirm or to undermine the relationship is less important, finally, than the fact that his attitude is equivocal, that at this point his normative irony dissolves into the strictly descriptive irony of his narrator. Significantly, communication breaks down between author and reader in Isherwood's attempt to articulate what is potentially the book's one unqualified ideal, for, as we have already noted, Isherwood is more anxious than able to embody or perhaps to believe in the genuine forms of life. Something more is needed to construct blueprints of the future; Isherwood is on firmer ground in clearing away the debris.

III   The Truly Weak Man

He does so admirably in his treatment of the novel's two central characters, Eric Vernon and Edward Blake. The full force of Isherwood's ironic intent is nowhere more apparent than in the depiction of Eric's career, which in many ways retraces Philip Lindsay's. Eric is at his most impressive as the reader first encounters him, externally, through Anne's admiring eyes; but there is something disconcerting, even to the reader not yet attuned to the novel's image patterns, in the nature of her praise: "Yes, he really is my idea of a saint, Anne thought. ... You could have put him straight into the Bible, just as he was" (36). What Anne thinks she sees in him is an integrity so great that it inspires her family and their friends with a kind of fear, but her own reaction as she thinks about him—"a little uncomfortable and chilly" (37)—begins to give the reader a clue to the fact that Eric creates distance not because of his superiority but because of his lack of personal warmth and his inability to connect with others. The rest of the novel reveals gradually the chinks in the armor and the lonely, unhappy face beneath the mask.

The roots of Eric's problem are most fully exposed, as Philip's are, in his relations with his mother. Victimized by Lily's sadly sweet manner, her gentle repressiveness, and her air of weary and passive martyrdom, Eric is alternately prey to "a semi-superstitious fear . . . of meddling with the Past" (156) and to rebellious stirrings against the whole way of life she represents to him. These reactions lead in turn to constant remorse and guilt and to a cycle in which a ferocious sense of inadequacy alternates with feelings of impotent rage and hostility to produce the frustration symbolized by his stammer. Life with his cousins, he feels, offers a chance of "breaking out of his own clumsy identity" (172), but he is perversely attracted to or at any rate unable to transcend that identity.

It is while he is still, theoretically at least, in a state of potential that the reader has freest access to his mind and observes the vacillation indicated earlier in this chapter in his thoughts about Gatesley and Chapel Bridge. By itself, the contrast of the two villages serves to objectify Eric's choices; in its context (Eric is trying to express his perception of the differences in a poem), it provides an indication of the choice he will make. His comic difficulties in finding a rhyme underline his more serious difficulties in making up his mind; and his sudden realization, as he imagines himself to be a bit of magnetized metal drawn between the negative and the positive pole, that "a pin would never move between the poles at all, but fly to one and stick there" (173), predicts his own eventual flight to the negative.

His reaction when he arrives at Gatesley sets the seal on his future. It is, as far as Eric is concerned, the central symbolic moment of the novel; unseen by his cousins and their friends, he watches them for a few minutes joking and playing with each other, and then he turns away and starts back to the Hall. The scene emphasizes Eric's passivity and his role as observer. He is, clearly, the spectator of life, the perpetual outsider; he is attracted by the show of activity and movement but, like Philip, he guards himself from the involvement he fears by a self-defeating retreat into a private world of elaborate barriers and intricate defenses.

With time, the need for concealment grows. Torn between the claims of past and future, Lily and Mary, death and life, Eric makes increasingly wild stabs at finding an authentic existence, all the while moving relentlessly back to his starting point. Like Philip in his growing unawareness, Eric makes a wider and more significant circuit before he comes to rest, so that for a time his outwardly active life obscures the operation in him of what Auden refers to as the negative inversion of the will (*Collected Poetry*,

110); but his movement from Cambridge to the Communist party to, finally, the Catholic Church reveals gradually the disintegration of his personality and his will. Fittingly, he disappears altogether from the novel after the third section; and his absence from Part IV symbolizes his retreat, to all intents and purposes, from the human scene. The announcement of his conversion comes in a letter to Edward: "I have the most extraordinary feeling of peace. And you who know me will know what a lot that means" (291).

The irony is overwhelming: Eric is in full flight back to authority, to exactly the force, now in intensified form, from which he has been fleeing and against which he has been revolting. The final disposition of Eric is, then, another point of resemblance between him and Philip; but the problems Eric raises are more crucial in that they join public with private acts. Kingsley Amis's remark, apropos of the Auden Group's handling of political themes, that "in some ways these people were only conducting in public a personal vendetta against their parents . . . and one or two unsympathetic headmasters,"[6] is true enough insofar as it suggests the personal genesis of much 1930's writing; but the statement is wrong in its implication that these writers were unaware of what they were doing. *The Memorial* means to show the psychological causation of the political and, also, of the religious choices of the decade; in his study of Eric, Isherwood indicates his awareness that what seems to be a gesture of commitment may be simply the final refusal to make contact with life.

Isherwood's relation to his protagonist is made most apparent in *Lions and Shadows,* where he describes what he intended to do in the novel that became *The Memorial:* "It was to be about war: not the War itself, but the effect of the idea of 'War' on my generation. It was to give expression, at last, to my own 'War' complex" (296). War, in turn, is defined earlier in *Lions and Shadows* as "The Test. The test of your courage, of your maturity, of your sexual prowess: 'Are you really a Man?'" (76). Eric suffers, quite literally, from shame at not having fought in the war in which his father was killed; but his absorption in Isherwood's metaphoric notion of war is equally intense and more enduring. For Eric, life is consantly a test, a succession of bridges he never manages to cross; and one senses in Isherwood's portrait of him an exploration of and perhaps an attempt at exorcising his own obsessive concern with the idea of failure. Eric, however, is only one embodiment of the theme, which, despite Isherwood's contention that he was concerned with the effect of war on "my generation," receives its most crucial investigation in Edward Blake, who is, in his relation to Eric, the first of Isherwood's "doubles."

A number of touches create a symbolic tie between them; but the similarities are, more importantly, ones of character and attitude. Both, as boys, are misfits; both hate their schools; both develop, under the stress of their loneliness and fears, public personalities with which to disguise their inner lives; both suffer from a kind of romantic hero worship; and both are homosexual, although Eric, even when he recognizes that he is jealous of Edward's relationship with Maurice, is perhaps unwilling to accept fully the implications of his discovery.

The relations between Eric and Edward change in the course of their lives; and as Eric's initial feelings of jealousy, hostility, and distrust give way, there grows up between them, if not friendship, then a kind of mutual dependency and complicitousness in the face of the world that emphasizes the identity of their spirits. It is to Eric—"the only person I can trust" (56)—that Edward addresses his suicide note; and it is to Edward, who supplies the reader with his only information about Eric in the last section of the novel, that the younger man first reveals his decision to become a Catholic. By the end, then, there is little, in essentials, to choose between them; both represent what Isherwood calls in *Lions and Shadows* "the neurotic hero, The Truly Weak Man."[7] What Isherwood is describing is his idea for an unwritten novel that was to have been called *The North-West Passage;* and a little farther on he points out that two of the projected characters were meant to suggest "two halves or aspects of the same person," that one was to have been "an embodiment of [the other's] dream of himself as an epic character," but that both were in fact The Truly Weak Man, although one would "one day be lost in trying to force the North-West Passage," while the other would "never even dare attempt it"(211).

Isherwood is portraying, in other words, something very much like the relation between Edward and Eric: the active and the passive manifestations of the same disease. Eric's life is free of incident; he is the one who avoids the Passage altogether. Edward, on the other hand, is constantly attempting the huge northern circuit, but with no better results. Both are doomed to failure, and both in their different ways fail. Edward is shown from the first to be incapable of mastering life—his first scene is the one of his attempted suicide—but Eric is defeated, as it seems, only gradually. Edward, therefore, although the time scheme of the

novel allows the reader to see subsequently his earlier and later
efforts to give his life some meaning, has from the beginning a
determinate role. His function as Eric's double is, therefore, pre-
dictive as well as emphatic; and, if he remains to the end more
aware than Eric, that is only to show how much more abjectly the
latter succumbs to the defeat of the self.

Edward's place in *The Memorial* does not, however, depend
simply upon his connection with Eric. As Lily and Mary symbolize, for good or for evil, the potentialities of their world, Edward
symbolizes its actuality, life as it is rather than as it might be; he
is the mirror, then, not only for Eric but for all the others as well;
and in his frustrations and instability one sees reflected the
inadequacies of the whole Vernon family. The fact that he is not
related to them (he is the only major character who is not) and
that it is, therefore, hardly possible to explain away his attitudes
by reference to the Hall or any of the other ancestral curses that
haunt his friends helps to generalize his significance. Indeed, his
separateness gives him an almost mythic status in the novel: the
Fisher King of Isherwood's 1930's Waste Land. Most self-conscious and self-aware of all the characters, constantly mobile and
active, ultimately isolated from all the others, he epitomizes in his
own life the sterility and aridity of all the lives in the book. In his
search for something that will excite him and make his life meaningful, in his efforts to allay his boredom and restlessness, there is
a paradigmatic quality—the attempt of the self to break out of its
limitations and find a resting place in an unsatisfactory world.

As for the results of this attempt, the book makes them clear in
its last pages, where in a comic decrescendo more subtle than its
counterpart in *All the Conspirators*, Isherwood makes his final
comment not only on Edward but, through him, on all the other
characters in the novel as well. Beginning with Margaret's sentimental letter—filled with muzzy seasonal cheer, breathing tolerance of Edward's homosexuality, and predicting for them, against
all the evidence of their previous lives, a happy although sexless
future—and moving on to Eric's unctuous announcement of his
conversion, and then ending with Edward's encounter with Franz,
the latest but certainly not the last of his young men, the closing
scene exposes as inadequate, one by one, the various solutions—
love, religion, and sex—offered to him. And Isherwood leaves him,
among all the empty gestures and pious statements, the failures to
understand and to connect, more alone than ever in a world that
promises no hope, no change, no way out. As the chapter focuses
on Edward's various relationships in turn, words become less and

less adequate to their job, until, in the conversation with Franz, communication breaks down altogether. Weary, mocking, sophisticated, Edward continues to do his tricks, covering the void with one more game, while the vain, animal-like, materialistic young German, through his misinterpretations of Margaret's letter ("Doesn't 'dear' mean expensive?" [293]) and Edward's scar ("Why should you shoot yourself? You've got money. . . . Wasn't it in the War?" [293–94]) reduces affection to money and the war to the level of suicide.

The whole of the last chapter is reductive: as the various themes of the novel are recapitulated, the reader is made aware of a kind of stiffening, the final despiritualization and trivializing of a world already half dead. The several references to Christmas, with which the chapter opens, serve (whether as conventional references to birth and communion or as the last instances of the book's use of religious images to suggest rigidity and negation) only to underscore the triumph of death over life; and the final words of the novel throw into high ironic relief the moral chaos of all the lives in it: " 'You know,' said Franz, very serious and evidently repeating something he had heard said by his elders: 'that War . . . it ought never to have happened' " (294). Nothing has been learned; nothing will be changed. The hollow commandments of the "elders" continue to reverberate through the Waste Land, where the sins of the fathers are visited more and more pathetically on the generations that follow. The shadow of the "old gang" hangs over the present, and the barrenness of the present predicts the bleakness of the future.

As for Isherwood himself, although he implies the need for change, he offers little hope; the Thunder speaks, as it does in Eliot's poem, but there are no healing rains—no way that the characters can find to give, sympathize, and control. Edward's prominence not only in the final section but in the whole concluding time block of the novel casts over the landscape an enormous blight that makes clear the despair Isherwood feels in giving expression to his "War complex." As he moves from the anger of *All the Conspirators* to the irony of *The Memorial*, his vision broadens, but the tone of the exploration darkens.

If *All the Conspirators* deals with the struggle of the self against the "old gang," *The Memorial* is concerned, more broadly, with the struggle against the conditions of life which have been brought about in the first instance by the "old gang." Regeneration becomes more necessary, but also less likely, in what Auden referred to as "this country of ours where nobody is well."[8] Isherwood, responding to what he had seen in England, left the country in 1929 to begin for the next ten years a series of travels rivaling Edward Blake's in frequency and extent. The books that follow record the change of scene and the transformation of the Enemy into another shape altogether, but their theme remains very much the same, even as they undertake an increasingly hectic investigation into the ethics of salvation for a self henceforth sharing not only, more and more obviously, Isherwood's past but also, for the first time, his name.

CHAPTER *4*

Private Faces and Public Places

"THEY HAVE been great egotists," Virginia Woolf wrote, referring to the 1930's writers associated with Auden and indicating not their weakness but their strength: "When everything is rocking round one, the only person who remains comparatively stable is oneself. . . . So they wrote about themselves."[1] Products of the middle-class training and the expensive educations against which they revolted—in themselves as in the "old gang"—these inhabitors of "The Leaning Tower," as Mrs. Woolf called them, desired above all "to be whole; to be human . . . to be down on the ground with the rest of human kind";[2] they desired, that is to say, some accommodation between self and world. The larger part of her essay is meant to show how and why they failed, despite their strenuous attempts to subvert the ivory tower of the 1920's, to achieve the ideal of commitment that is associated with their own period. As V. S. Pritchett put it: "The aesthete gave place to the reporter, to a figure who was really no more 'in life' than the aesthete had been. The reporter merely *seemed* more committed because he got around. He had put the ivory tower on wheels."[3]

But the 1930's writers were far from unaware of their own conflicts and failures: Spender's label for his friends, "The Divided Generation,"[4] Auden's and Day Lewis's poems of internal struggle and doubt, and the reiterated discontents of the protagonist of *Lions and Shadows* all substantiate and generally precede Mrs. Woolf's observation that the Tower dwellers were caught, as Day Lewis put it, between "two worlds at war."[5] Most of them would probably have agreed that they did their best, if not, as they then thought, their most valuable work when they took as their subject matter the "comparatively stable" self.

What Mrs. Woolf's account fails to reckon with is, on the one hand, how much more fluid and undependable even the self is for the young men of the 1930's than it was for her own generation and, on the other, how much more inextricable are the relations between self and world. Her essay seems to suggest at times too strict a division of 1930's writing into the socially conscious and

53

the esthetic. One can easily grant that the former is too often dominated by "the pedagogic, the didactic, the loud speaker strain,"[6] without however seeing the latter as somehow *hors de combat.* I have already referred to Michael Roberts's statement in which the self-absorption of the New Country group is seen to be both moral and therapeutic. The retreat from the world is, in this context, an attempt, not always fully conscious perhaps, to recover the world through a more rigorous and honest understanding of the self. It would be futile to pretend that the attempt is usually or even often successful, but it is obvious that the best work of the period is both autobiographical and "engaged."

What is important in understanding Isherwood—who, except in the plays he wrote with Auden and in some of his essays, represents the least tendentious of the 1930's authors—is the degree to which writing about the self or themselves was for the poets and novelists of the period a process of dynamic exploration, the means of discovering rather than simply of expressing value. The consequences are sometimes, as Mrs. Woolf maintains, largely confusion; more frequently, they manifest themselves either in an overemphatic attempt to establish contact with the world, or in a characteristic equivocation, an ironic hesitancy about the very values being expressed. In all these cases, the moral visions of these writers' novels and poems are with varying intensity rendered ambiguous and occasionally subverted by the techniques used to articulate them.

The dangers of accepting these authors' own conceptions of what they intended or accomplished in their writings can be illustrated by reference to *The Last of Mr. Norris* (1935). Isherwood has several times referred to the heartlessness of the book's protagonist, as if he discovered only after the fact of creating him how morally insensitive William Bradshaw was. In the preface to *The Berlin Stories* (dated 1954), for example, he writes: "Only a very young and frivolous foreigner, I thought, could have lived in such a place and found it amusing. Hadn't there been something youthfully heartless in my enjoyment of the spectacle of Berlin in the early thirties, with its poverty, its political hatred and its despair?" (x).[7] And yet the impact of the novel depends precisely upon the reader's increasing awareness of Bradshaw's failings and upon his willingness to render judgment on him. The problem is, of course, to discover whatever ethical bias the rhetoric of the book itself enforces, to credit "the core of norms and choices" to which Booth gives the name of "the implied author"[8] rather than the historical Isherwood who is ultimately responsible for the work.

What is suggested here is that the Isherwood who figures in his friends' autobiographies is related to but by no means identical either with the protagonists and the narrators who in his next four books bear his name (which is, in full, Christopher William Bradshaw-Isherwood) or with the creator whose vision informs these books. For Spender, reporting Auden's opinion, Isherwood "held no opinions whatever about anything. He was wholly and simply interested in people. He did not like or dislike them, judge them favourably or unfavourably. He simply regarded them as material for his Work";[9] but, for the reader, he must be inevitably no more and no less than the total implication of the novels' various techniques. The difficulty is compounded by Isherwood's easy movement, as in the statement quoted in the previous paragraph, from his character to himself. Despite various disclaimers (" 'Christopher Isherwood' is a convenient ventriloquist's dummy, nothing more"[10]), it is difficult to believe that for Isherwood the separation was at all so easy or so complete. Furthermore, it is hard to ignore an author's decision, whatever literary justification it may have, to give to the narrators of half of his books his own name or to overlook what is otherwise implied by the repeated image of mirrors in the novels: the concern, the curiosity, the search for order and understanding that the obsessive transformation of autobiography into art suggests.

The Williams and Christophers of the books between *Mr. Norris* and *Prater Violet* are, one comes to feel, projections of Isherwood's own uncertainties. They are not only artisitic ends but also the means to the discovery and stabilizing of the self. (What delight he takes throughout his career in ringing changes on his name: Herr Issyvoo, Curaçao Chris, Y Hsiao Wu, and other less exotic metamorphoses of the basic formula of identity!) As these characters move between the public life and the private, between the passive eye and the self-conscious "I," some advance is made, not necessarily in their own awareness but, at however submerged a level, in Isherwood's; and the tone and concerns of each successive book reflects the growth. "My work is all part of an autobiography,"[11] Isherwood has admitted; and his protagonists can be viewed as so many points which, joined, form the line of his development from the anger of his first novel through the increasingly ironic scrutiny of his several alter egos during the 1930's— a process largely, as in the early works of Joyce and Forster, of rejection and repudiation—to the gradual discovery, in the works beginning with *Prater Violet*, of the "real self," the Atman, the final answer to the claims of the ego.

But this is to anticipate: in the period 1935–45 there is in Isherwood's writings a radical interaction of life and fiction, a symbi-

otic partnership between the raw materials of the one and the
tentative normative explorations of the other. In the growing disenchantment that these years reveal, leading to the crisis that
Isherwood has discussed most explicitly in *An Approach to
Vedanta*, one senses the use of art as exorcism: what is purged is
the compulsive need, symbolic and actual, psychological and
physical, to travel. *The Last of Mr. Norris* opens with William
Bradshaw on a train, completing the first stage of his—and of
Isherwood's—journey.

I   The Doubleness of Mr. Norris

The Last of Mr. Norris, whatever its covert relation to its author's private and instinctive life, is in most respects a carefully
controlled, calculated piece of fiction. Isherwood's own description of it—"a sort of glorified shocker; not unlike the productions
of my cousin Graham Greene"[12]—suggests the novel's principal
strategy. Through the use of a narrator committed to a sequential
and unobtrusive relation of the facts of his own earlier life, the
novel aims to confuse, mislead, and mystify the reader, to trap
him, as the protagonist is trapped, in repeated failures of perception and, more importantly, of evaluation. The reader is supplied, most often by the narrator, sometimes by the author
himself, with clues to proper understanding; but Isherwood's intention is that these clues, like Gide's *fausses pistes,* pass only
gradually from the realm of empirical data to that of significant
fact, that they achieve their full ethical value only in retrospect.
The success of the novel, both in creating its esthetic pattern and
in establishing its moral position, depends upon the reader's
recognition, only slightly prior to the protagonist's, of his previous
obtuseness. In other words, he must, or Isherwood must make him,
run with the impercipient hare and ride, however late in starting,
with the ironic hounds.

Both the narrative technique and the characterization of the
book are at least superficially analogous to those of the mystery
novel. The plot—spare, selective, mounting in intensity—provides
the forward thrust of the book, engaging the reader on the most
primitive levels of expectancy and suspense and then awakening
him with its element of surprise to the sophisticated implications
of the spy drama he has been witnessing. But if the narrative
movement invites, at least for a long period, indiscriminate absorption in the book, the leading characters, rendered as they are
with persistent and teasing ambiguity, demand sustained attention
and intelligence. For the "who-done-it" of the detective novel,

Mr. Norris substitutes the "what-is-he" of the modern *roman d'a-venture*. The question is most insistent with respect to the titular hero of the book himself.

From the start, there is about the stranger on the train not only an air of mystery but also, more tangibly, an effect of doubleness, a comic, almost grotesque quality of incongruity. The nearly but not quite perfect wig, to which William's attentive and fascinated eyes stray repeatedly, becomes the major expression of the attempt, naïve, as it seems at first, to disguise reality with an elaborately contrived appearance. Indeed, everything about Arthur Norris, above all the elaborate ritual of the dressing table at which William comes eventually to serve as a bemused acolyte, suggests that he is not what he seems. But the moral judgment, which might be expected to follow upon this perception of accumulated and habitual discrepancy, is neutralized for Bradshaw by what seems the transparency of the intended deception; even Arthur's evasiveness is accepted, if not always without comment, without prejudice. And so with the reader: the form of the first-person narrative exacts from him an understandable willingness to credit the sensory details with which he is presented and involves him in the more puzzling process of analysis upon which the protagonist immediately enters; inevitably, although less logically, he adopts as well William's conjectures and surmises about Arthur's character and affairs.

What makes for Bradshaw's amused acceptance of his bizarre friend is his belief that he is dealing with an essentially timid, childlike soul who is very much at the mercy of those around him and who, by contrast with William's disapproving acquaintances, is particularly and attractively vulnerable. This ingenuousness—along with the charm that displays itself in the little delicacies to Fräulein Schroeder, in the old-fashioned, 1890's wit, and in the obvious desire to please—supplies the foreground of William's portrait of Norris and helps to blur the significance of the details of the latter's tastes and habits as they gradually come into focus.

This separation of matter from manner (or is it the belated recognition of their inextricable relationship?) is after the fact. It is sober reason, disabused of Mr. Norris's pervasive charm, that recognizes in him a propensity to see life as a game, people as instruments, and injustice as an offense against good taste. In one of his notable utterances about the police, he remarks: "The very cut of their uniforms offends me, and the German helmets are not only hideous but somehow rather sinister" (58). Essentially nomadic, a sort of cosmopolitan and unconscious Cain or Wandering

Jew, as the book's imagery suggests at one point, Arthur is in the final analysis a man without values, self-interest excepted, a paradigm of the detached and esthetic observer.

In the light of this disillusioned assessment, based as it is on facts readily and almost from the start available to the reader, the question once again presents itself of why, even allowing for our curiosity and fascination, we accept Arthur Norris and allow ourselves to be charmed by him. Part of the answer, as has already been suggested, lies in the point of view of the novel. But are we simply the dupes of Isherwood's rhetoric? It hardly seems that that can be the whole of the explanation: whatever suspension of disbelief a work of literature demands, it is on difficult ground when it asks the reader totally to put aside, more so still when it asks him to contravene, his values. To a degree, at least, our failure is moral rather than intellectual, an error inherent in the quality not of our literary response but in the more general response we bring from life to art.

Paradoxically, what is at issue here is an attitude that sees itself as, and often is, commendable—the particularly modern, enlightened attitude toward the private life. A man's personal preferences, we tend to feel, are his own business: if Arthur chooses to make himself up, if he enjoys being whipped, well ... that's his affair. Fräulein Schroeder, sewing quietly while the sounds of pleasure issue from her lodger's room next door, comments: "I do hope Herr Norris won't injure himself. He ought to be more careful at his time of life" (99). The remark, less consciously and less methodically than those of Forster, for example, expresses, at least on the surface, that sense of tolerance which is a central feature of liberal humanism. "The doctrine of *laisser-faire*," as Forster puts it, "is the only one that seems to work in the world of the spirit."[13]

Arthur is himself the apostle of tolerance. After his betrayal of William, or after its discovery, his attempt at justification involves an appeal to open-mindedness and relativism. The treachery to Bradshaw, to the Baron, and to the Communist party, which is disclosed in the aftermath of the "Swiss project," provides the turning point in the reader's and in William's understanding of Mr. Norris. But these revelations are in fact less startling in telling us something new—specific actions apart, what is there that the sordid affair can tell us about Norris that is not already implicit in his attitude toward individuals, causes, and countries?—than in placing what we know in a new context. Suddenly we are made to realize the public consequences of Arthur's private life; and, despite his disingenuous protestations that he will not "mix per-

sonal with business relationships" (135), we perceive that his public and private lives are in fact the same.

Other characters in the book, notably the pathetic Pregnitz,
attempt more honestly than Norris to separate the two lives; but
Isherwood's lesson is that the effort is a futile one. The point is
made in the second chapter of the novel, long before its import
can conceivably be grasped by the reader or by Bradshaw (it is at
least possible that the narrator himself is never aware of its significance), and by way of what appears to be a piece of purely infor-
mational narration. When William, on his first visit to Norris's
apartment, notices that there are two front doors, with two name-
plates engraved: *"Arthur Norris. Private"* and *"Arthur Norris. Import and Export,"* the suggestion of a definite division between
the inner and outer lives is made. This impression is dispelled as
soon as the door is opened: "I noticed immediately I was inside,"
William reports with surprise but without further comment, "the
Private side of the entrance hall was divided from the Export side
only by a thick hanging curtain" (13).

What the reader learns as he proceeds through the book is the
appositeness of this description of the two rooms that are in fact
one to an understanding of the character of Norris, in whom the
apparent, contrary to expectations, is in fact the real. The reader
recognizes, as the perverse conclusion to his exercise in detection,
that behind the curtain there is nothing at all or, more accurately,
only an extension of the already visible. Ultimately, the most
frightening fact about the seemingly mysterious Arthur is that
there *is* nothing to hide; that, in the most fundamental sense, he
has no identity more complex than that which he reveals at first
sight. There are secrets but no depths; the symbolic divider is only
the tolerant opacity of the world ready to acquiesce in any devia-
tions from its own norms so long as they remain nameless and
without visible social consequence. *Mr. Norris* is the slow unfold-
ing of the psychology of a monster, egoistic, conscienceless, totally
unaware of the evil he is doing. But it is, even more, a moral study
of the nature and consequences of amorality, an attempt, in the
final analysis, not to enlighten but to educate the reader.

II   Mr. Norris and His Doubles

Part of the reaction against the Ivory Towerism of the 1920's is
apparent in the fact that so many of the writers of the following
decade deal in some form with the relations between the individual and those external events, which, because of their more
general and diffused significance, appear at first sight remote and

even alien to the individual's concerns. For a poet like Spender, the problem is to show what happens to the private self in the light of the public one; for Isherwood, as we have seen, it is to indicate the public consequences of private acts. Inevitably, then, Mr. Norris's drama and those of all the characters in the book are played out against a larger social and political background—specifically, the coming to power of the Nazi party in the chaotic Germany of the 1930's—which is increasingly seen to mirror and finally to be the outcome of their deeds of commission and omission. The parallels are numerous and pointed: between Arthur's delight in flagellation and the Germans' enthusiastic reception of Hitler; between the difficult and sometimes bogus communication that marks the dealings of individuals and the pervasive inflation of the German language (which provides a *moral* justification for Isherwood's own severely understated and ironic style); between Kuno's dreams of a desert island populated with handsome, athletic youths and the current Aryan myth; between, finally, the Berliners' acceptance of immorality and their "profoundly indifferent" (110) reaction to the violence and maneuverings of the political struggle.

Arthur, of course, is the central point of reference; he gives William, in his conversations with him, the feeling that they are "speaking similar but distinct languages" (3); and he provides, in his soberly delivered credo on "the privilege of the richer but less mentally endowed members of the community to contribute to the upkeep of people like myself" (39), a parodic but equivalent restatement of the *Übermensch* mentality. But, in kind if not in degree, the others in the book are also implicated.

Stylistically, the novel contrives to draw our attention to the underlying similarities through a virtual menagerie of animal images applied to the characters, major and minor alike. Between the first chapter of the novel, in which Mr. Norris and William part at the Zoo Station, to the last pages, where the former refers to his erstwhile secretary as "the reptile" (190), a collection of lions, tigers, cobras, cats, birds, and fish—to single out only the most recurrent figures—roams through the book, obliquely establishing the truth of what lies beneath the overly civilized exterior of Berlin life. In this animal-like world, the cosmopolitan jungle code is severely utilitarian; the inhabitants, like the procuress Olga, the pimp Otto, the journalist Helen Pratt, who is "out to get the facts" (180), and, inevitably, Norris himself, are so many combatants in the struggle to be among the fittest who survive.

Common to all of the characters is a disengagement from human relations that manifests itself in the novel's most characteristic facial expression: the smile. Like the playfulness of Conrad's Axel Heyst, the insistent and equivocal gesture underlines, even more strongly than it does in *The Memorial*, the essential lack of involvement that inhibits any genuine interchange in the book. The unwillingness or the inability, in any case the failure, to communicate is even more apparent at those rare moments when people do become personal—when, through force of circumstance, they are obliged to face one another—than at those more usual ones when they are prepared to avoid the menace of directness.

Throughout the book, any threat to the habitual displacement of emotion leads, therefore, to expression in terms of abrupt and physical force, the instinctive and defensive reaction of a creature taken unawares. In Berlin "hate exploded suddenly, without warning, out of nowhere" (86). In the meeting of Bradshaw and Schmidt, the latter's purposefully offensive composure is shattered completely when William, personal for a moment, asks him if he is ill: "His oily, smiling sneer stiffened into a tense mask of hatred. He had utterly lost control of himself. ... His hysterical fury infected me suddenly. Stepping back, I flung the door to with a violent slam" (121).

But it is Fräulein Schroeder's boiler that gives final expression to the unnaturalness of human relations in the novel: perpetually ready to explode, it threatens, in the midst of William's abnormally restrained confrontation with Arthur after the Swiss affair, to blow to bits. The touch is Dickensian—the inanimate taking over and distorting in a comical but frightening reversal of roles the discarded functions of the animate. And the point, a favorite one of the psychologically oriented 1930's writers is that, as the narrator of *Lions and Shadows* writes, quoting the gospel of Homer Lane: "There is only one sin: disobedience to the inner law of our own nature. The results of this disobedience show themselves in crime or in disease" (300). In the violent, sick, and, for all its aura of vice and freedom, repressed world of *Mr. Norris*, "the whole city [lies] under an epidemic of discreet, infectious fear" (181).

The most uncompromising expression of the general malady is Norris's secretary, Schmidt. Without the redeeming wit, manners, or good looks of the other characters, he is unique in revealing immediately and unmistakably the essential inner truth about himself. Significantly, he elicits from Bradshaw at their first meeting what is probably the protagonist's single, unqualified assertion of personal disapproval in the book. Arthur's references to his secre-

tary as a snake suggest at first that Schmidt is an embodiment of
the devil; but Isherwood's recent description of him as "quite
literally a familiar,"[14] although it does not preclude the infernal
associations, is more to the point.

Schmidt is, in fact, Norris's double,[15] the ugly and charmless
projection of everything Arthur less obviously is, his "right hand"
(16), the inevitable effect of his cause. As in Auden's poem, "Crisis," in which "We" are shown to be responsible for the "Terrible
Presences" (*Collected Poetry,* 169) that afflict "us," so in *Mr. Norris,* the malignant secretary functions as the visible form of the
disease that is abroad. In the final pages of the novel, where the
too insistent irony is such as to make incomprehensible Walter
Allen's comment that "Isherwood makes no moral judgment of
[Norris],"[16] the identity of Arthur and Schmidt is complete. The
one fleeing, the other pursuing, in a circuitous journey whose
stages Norris describes as Paradise, Purgatory, and the Inferno,
the two men end in a "new partnership ... doomed to walk the
Earth together" (191). Norris himself remains sublimely unconscious to the end; but the reader, presented with his indignant
comments on the Nazis, who "are nothing more or less than criminals" (189), is ready to recognize the final orchestration of the
basic theme: the criminal is Arthur himself; the public and the
private sicknesses are one.

If virtue is to be found anywhere in the novel, it is among the
Communists, in the anonymous rank and file[17] and more particularly in Ludwig Bayer. At the party meeting William attends, he
is struck by the attitude of the audience, which is, as he half-
perceives, so different from his own: "They were attentive but not
passive. They were not spectators. They participated, with a curious, restrained passion" (48). But, as in all of Isherwood's prewar
novels, no ideal emerges quite without reservation; and those who
are good in *The Last of Mr. Norris* are generally stupid. In part,
at least, the total political naïvete of a Fräulein Schroeder, the
gullibility of an Otto, or the credulousness of the crowd applaud-
ing Arthur cancel out, in a book predicated upon the connection
between shrewdness and survival, their otherwise attractive enthusiasm and warmth.

The case of Bayer is more complex. Apparently as astute as he
is dedicated, he establishes himself, when he first appears in the
novel as its most vigorous character and, when he is last heard of
—in Helen Pratt's gruesome report of his death—as its chief martyr. The descriptions of him suggest energy and activity but also
concentration and control. Difficulty arises from the fact that the

verbal texture of the novel implicates Bayer in the network of images and gestures that defines the other characters as well (note his "animal eyes" [62] and his constant smile). Moreover, the novel presents in other ways as well evidence for differing interpretations of the Communist leader. Bayer's tolerance, his conscious manipulations and outmaneuverings of Arthur, his surprising statement to William, after exposing Norris's duplicity —"Mind, I have not said this against him as a man; the private life is not our concern" (157)—all suggest his participation in the dominant ethical assumptions of the book. On the other hand, his gratuitous rescue of Bradshaw, and, above all, the fact that his actions are performed in the service of a cause to which his allegiance is complete, put him in a class apart from the others.

The problem is one of deciding whether Isherwood's intention —if it is in this case a matter of deliberate intention at all—is to qualify the favorable picture of Bayer or to undermine his narrator. Either alternative is possible. The point once again is that, awareness apart, the stringency of Isherwood's irony and, consequently, of the formal devices he uses to express it is such that the possibilities of affirmation are far more limited than those of negation. Isherwood's vocabulary, like his syntax, is an instrument of exclusion; and those stylistic effects of understatement and disconnection described in an earlier chapter militate in themselves against the direct and unequivocal expression of value. Ultimately, it becomes clear, the decision about Bayer rests on a prior assumption, made with the difficulties of Isherwood's technique in mind, about the character and perceptiveness of the narrator, all the more so since the point of view imposes an external approach to all of the characters except Bradshaw. If the narrator is "reliable," Bayer must be seen at least in part as a victim of the forces he is fighting; if he is not, then the most sustained irony of the novel is at Bradshaw's expense; and the most radical failure is his own.

But failure is a relative matter in a character who is presented as changing and developing. All of Isherwood's first-person novels, whatever their ostensible subjects, concern the education of their narrators. As a result, the Bradshaw who describes the events of the book, however like or unlike the author whose tool he is, is not the same person as the William whom the reader first meets in 1930. Anachronistically speaking, the latter is a continuation of the Christopher who sets off for Berlin in the final pages of *Lions and Shadows*, still a traveler, passing through life with a wary and disillusioned eye but ready at any moment to fall under the spell of another Mortmere. In Arthur Norris he finds, suddenly come to life, a figure from that mad village transposed on to the international scene. But, if Arthur inspires Bradshaw's esthetic daydreaming and, in his apparent pliability and dependency, William's "affectionate protectiveness" (9), still more Arthur encourages, only partly through his systematic flattery, Bradshaw's desired image of himself as a sophisticated, liberal, and emancipated man of the world. More to the point, Arthur offers William, as the reader at least recognizes, a grotesque but not inaccurate mirror image.

If Schmidt is Arthur's counterpart, the concretion of all that he actually is, then Norris, at least potentially, is Bradshaw's. Symbolically, the connection is made a number of times, but the more important resemblances are a question of shared attitudes and responses to life. Like Arthur, William lacks warmth, has no real human relations, and finds life most palatable when viewed as a game; in short, he is another uninvolved spectator of life. It is impossible not to be struck by William's constant lack of reaction, whether to the spectacle of Olga's whipping Arthur; to the Baron's sexual advances, which neither surprise nor bother him; or to the discovery he thinks he makes that he is being used by Bayer to spy on Norris: "I felt angry," he says, untypically, and then adds, more in character, "and at the same time rather amused. After all, one couldn't blame them" (67).

What change there is in William comes as a result of what he learns, or now first fully admits to himself, about Arthur's part in the Swiss affair. For despite his characteristic detachment of himself from the event and despite his failure to carry through a genuine confrontation with his friend (the timely eruption of Fräulein Schroeder's boiler effectively closes the scene between them, and in the aftermath the status quo is restored), William does give some evidence of development. His awareness that the reconciliation is an inadequate substitute for the honesty and frankness that ought to have been forthcoming and his concern for Arthur's feelings reveal a new understanding and a heretofore unfelt humanity. But the empathy remains exceptional, and knowledge is in itself no guarantee of emotional maturity. The William who acquiesces in the old relationship and who is presumably to be equated with the narrator is, on the evidence of the rest of the novel, in no way substantially different from the foreigner newly arrived in Berlin.

As in *Lions and Shadows*, the dramatic irony of the book depends upon a disparity in experience and perception between the two but not upon any radical variations in their characters. Clearly, the very telling of the story indicates the narrator's awareness of the moral flaws in Arthur; but it does not follow that, in seeing Norris for what he is, he necessarily recognizes all of the implications of what he has done, or that he apprehends the connections that the book as a whole implies between the public and private lives.

One turns to Isherwood again for guidelines; but, as was earlier suggested, there is in this final matter of determining the reliability of the narrator an insufficiency of rhetorical clues. The temptation, certainly, is to see in certain of the symbolic details and correspondences (the two rooms or the boiler, for example) not Bradshaw's but Isherwood's hand and to detect in these a judgment on the narrator more devastating, if more covert, than that rendered on the protagonist. But it is difficult to be sure; only at two points does there seem to be some definite evidence pointing to Bradshaw's incomplete development. In the final paragraphs of the novel the narrator's moralistic distaste suggests that at the least he has missed the resemblances between himself and Norris. Much earlier, during the scene at the Communist rally, William feels, in response to the "passion," the "strength of purpose" (48) of the audience, a sense of his own apartness: "I stood outside it. One day, perhaps, I should be with it, but never of it" (48–49).

The remark, whether the narrator is here simply articulating William's thought or, for once, commenting upon it, apparently charts the extent of possible growth in Bradshaw. It is clear that he is not, even as he looks back on his adventure, "of it"; whether he is, in that significantly ambiguous phrase, "with it," remains doubtful. Isherwood explains in his preface to *The Berlin Stories* that *The Last of Mr. Norris* is "a title which should be followed by a very faint question mark" (vi), and the suggestion holds good for the novel as well. The original, English title, *Mr. Norris Changes Trains*, directs the reader to an open and hypothetical future, and that is where he must in fact look. There remains a real possibility that the indeterminacy of the novel reflects Isherwood's own irresolutions. Certainly, the problem of detachment and commitment that William poses is Isherwood's too; and his explorations of it continue and deepen both in the books that follow and, as his autobiographical comments on his conversion testify, in his life as well.

CHAPTER *5*

The Exiles

I The Camera's Eye

To enter the world of *Goodbye to Berlin* (1939) is immediately to become aware of the intransigence of objects. Everywhere in Fräulein Schroeder's apartment and in the streets outside is the decaying inheritance of the past, heavy, old, shabby and dirty; everywhere there are reminders of an earlier Germany, Prussian, Gothic, and belligerent, the legacy of "tarnished valuables and second-hand furniture of a bankrupt middle class" (1). But objects are not simply ponderous dead weight and obstructiveness. Throughout the novel, "things" are vaguely threatening (the halberds in Christopher's room, for example, which are joined, innocuously enough, to form his hatstand, are nonetheless "heavy and sharp enough to kill" [2])—until, in the final section of the book, they have become the visible sign of Nazi domination and violence: the last stage in the unholy metamorphosis of men into machines of destruction.

As in Dickens's novels, in this one by Isherwood the hostility of things is symbolic most importantly of a failure in personal integrity and personal relations. Objects possess what Dorothy Van Ghent has brilliantly called "demonic aptitude,"[1] a perverse life of their own in an otherwise dehumanized universe. In Isherwood's world, the quality of dehumanization is made immediately apparent through the syntax of the book's opening sentence—"From my window the deep massive solemn street" (1)—which contains neither subject nor verb. The "I," whose conspicuous absence implies both the theme and the technique of the novel, is usurped by an eye, activity by observation—as the most famous statement in Isherwood's work which follows shortly, makes clear: "I am a camera, with its shutter open, quite passive, recording not thinking" (1). It needs to be said that Christopher's remark is neither a revelation about Isherwood and his artistic methods, as some critics have maintained,[2] nor an indication that the narrator is as neutral and insensate as the camera to which he compares himself.

Passive though Christopher may be in his perception, he is hardly without emotion and even passion: "A Berlin Diary (Autumn 1930)," in particular its opening sections, is in fact dense with feelings of loneliness, discomfort, and frustration. Between the attentive, outward-directed gaze of Christopher's camera-eye and the essential privacy of his feelings there is, however, a wide gap. What he lacks is not emotion but the ability to project emotion beyond himself, to relate to and connect with others.

The two "Diaries" in *Goodbye to Berlin* are unusually (but understandably, given their form) revealing in their presentation of the interior shape of the narrator's affective being. In response to the objects and people he sees in his room and from his window, there wells up in him a sense of being simultaneously shut out and shut in. Confined by his foreignness in a strange city, he is excluded by the whistling, "lascivious and private and sad" (1), of young men to their girls in the rooms that line his street. The problem, then, that dominates the first of the "Berlin Diaries" is the usual one of Isherwood's novels, though in more exacerbated form, of the self acutely uncomfortable in the world of time and space, a world that is both its prison and its external form.

The reader is not, however, allowed to dwell very long upon this problem or to involve himself directly with Christopher's personal obsessions. The movement of this opening section of *Goodbye to Berlin* is centrifugal: each of its parts progresses as it appears, farther and farther out and away from its narrator-center and ends on an absurd and ironic note, as far removed as possible, it would seem, from the private anguish of the first few pages.

In this sense, "A Berlin Diary (Autumn 1930)" represents a kind of miniature of *Goodbye to Berlin* as a whole—"this short loosely-connected sequence of diaries and sketches,"[3] as Isherwood has called it—except that the novel itself returns with more symmetry to its protagonist at its close. Indeed, in this last of his 1930's novels, Isherwood seems to have found the perfect structural equivalent for his ironic vision of life as fragmented and discontinuous. But the point can be pushed too far: if the narrator does in fact see life in this way, the author is, as usual, creating a more coherent pattern behind his back. *Goodbye to Berlin* has, of course, a different kind of form from that of *Mr. Norris;* more complex and more symbolic, denser in texture, it is obviously more heterogeneous than the earlier book.

Isherwood has himself explained the differences between the two kinds of novels he has written: "One is a real constructed novel.... In fact you might say *All the Conspirators, The*

Memorial, I suppose *Mr. Norris* and *The World in the Evening* are constructed novels; and that *Goodbye to Berlin* and *Prater Violet* ... are, as it were, portraits. I've constantly used a rather stupid and pretentious sounding phrase, 'dynamic portraits', but what I mean is a portrait that grows. ... And by successive stages, the viewer is encouraged to look deeper and deeper into the picture, until finally it looks completely different to him."[4]

"Dynamic portrait" is, in fact, a better description of *Goodbye to Berlin* than the too modest "loosely-connected sequence"; the phrase provides a central and emerging focus for the novel in the character of Christopher and supplies an explanation of the reader's necessarily complex reactions to the characters and events of the book. Early in the first "Berlin Diary," Fräulein Schroeder tells anecdotes of the "really well connected and well educated— proper gentlefolk" (3) who have been her boarders. One's initial reaction to these ghosts of the past, who have left in various stains around the room the marks of their former tenancy, is to be amused—so long as one maintains Fräulein Schroeder's esthetic distance and regards Herr Noeske and the others as simply figures in a story. But another perspective is possible, and indeed, required by the texture of the "Diary" as a whole and by the reader's own inevitable awareness of the discrepancy between matter and manner: seeing in this alternative way, penetrating the surface and supplying the missing comments and emotional resonance, one is suddenly aware of how sordid and depressing it all is.

And so it is with the book generally. As one follows the Berlin scene through Christopher's all-observant eyes and listens to his fluent, ostensibly uninvolved voice bringing its landscape to life, one accepts easily enough the camera image, thereby relegating Christopher to the background of the novel and allowing oneself, as when turning the pages of a photograph album, to be casually interested and entertained. But to refuse to take the narrator at his own word, to see, in the lack of comment, disenchantment and, in detachment, fear and uncertainty—to become aware, in short, of Christopher as the cynosure of the novel and of his buried life as its principal subject—is to come to know Isherwood's strategy and to recognize what V. S. Pritchett, with somewhat different intent, refers to as "the interaction of the reporter and the artist at its most delicate."[5]

II The Lost

At the same time, the best way of beginning to understand Christopher (and the underlying pattern of the book) is through an examination of the four characters who occupy the foreground of the work. Sally Bowles, Peter Wilkinson, Otto Nowak, and Bernhard Landauer are all among "The Lost," a group that Isherwood defines in the preface to *The Berlin Stories* as including "not only The Astray and The Doomed—referring tragically to the political events in Germany and our epoch—but also 'The Lost' in quotation marks—referring satirically to those individuals whom respectable society shuns in horror" (v). It can be argued that Peter and particularly Bernhard fit more easily into the first, Sally and Otto into the second of Isherwood's groups; but a more subtle distinction can be made between them, one based upon the use of animal imagery, which appears almost as frequently in *Goodbye to Berlin* as in *Mr. Norris*. But in the later book the reference is not simply or foremost to the predatory world of uneasy survival, but to a certain mental set that is most obvious in Otto and Sally and that is missing in Bernhard and Peter.

According to this distinction, the animals are the preeminently adaptable, those who, being generally free from worry, anxiety, and guilt, feel very much at home in their worlds. Their opposites, who are obviously in the line of the leading characters of Isherwood's first two novels, are the unadaptable, the hostile, those who evidence a constant and profound uneasiness with themselves and with their surroundings. In this form, the contrast may be misleading: the difference is one that has to do not with mental or moral health but with consciousness; sensing less, the animals suffer less. And it is another aspect of the book's doubleness that one may, as Christopher apparently often does, accept their vitality at face value and thereby mistake feverish sickness for simple animation and high spirits.

Something of this reaction is apparent in Christopher's relationship with Sally Bowles. Most readers have found it easy to go along with the narrator in seeing Sally as the most attractive of his Berlin friends. Not that Christopher is at all deceived by her elaborate pretenses; he positively enjoys "watching her, like a performance at the theatre" (23). What Sally possesses, far more than Arthur Norris, with whom she shares a taste for disguise, makeup, and play-acting, is an ingenuous transparency that excuses, or at least mitigates, her occasional dishonesty and self-consciousness, her capacity for using people, and her elaborate artificiality. The main images that cluster around Sally suggest her childlikeness; and it is this quality—her essential innocence—along with the resilience that enables her to start again after each successive failure (and Sally fails everywhere and in everything) that make her so appealing.

But if Sally's charm is her naïveté, her strength derives from what may be thought of with some irony as her "sincerity," that is, her total capacity for self-deception and self-contradiction, her fertility in not only inventing but crediting her fantasies, her ability to accommodate herself to each new situation in turn with no apparent sense of the discontinuities of her life. To see Sally in this way is to stress, as the narrator, who both accepts and enjoys her, obviously does, what is vital, amusing, and plucky in her. Could one have reacted to Sally otherwise when her story first appeared as a separate volume in the late 1930's? Perhaps. For if one chooses to draw from Christopher's scattered and quickly moving observations—of Sally's hands, for example, which are "nervous, veined and very thin—the hands of a middle-aged woman" (29)—the conclusions he does not himself indicate, the picture becomes one not of animal exuberance but of very human pathos or, more ambiguously and complexly, of both together. In any case, this later response is an inevitable consequence of seeing her story within the total context of *Goodbye to Berlin* and particularly of comparing her, as one must, with Otto Nowak.

Even more egocentric and amoral, more "naturally and healthily selfish, like an animal" (87), Otto is also more the actor, an instinctive actor, like most of the rest of his family; but he possesses also a quality of malice and sadism of which Sally is at most only rarely and far less profoundly capable. If Otto is a kind of naïf too, unconsciously responsive only to the urgency of his own needs and desires, he is altogether a less appealing one—to the reader at least, if not necessarily to Christopher, whose attitude to him often seems to be conditioned by an unconscious or at least unstated homosexual attraction. A sexual sponger, indiscriminately prostituting himself to women and men, Otto is far less capable than Sally of sustaining a personal relation. But what finally makes him a more unsettling character is the quality of death that surrounds him. In his attempt at suicide, melodramatic and ineffectual as it is; in his easy adaptation to the sickly world of the sanatorium where he visits his mother; and, most of all, in his haunting and recurrent vision of an enormous black hand, whose next appearance, he tells Christopher, will mean his death, are revealed the disease which, despite surface appearances, is more advanced in him than in Sally and which gives the lie to the whole physical side of him.

If, then, Otto is an animal, he is a sick animal; and his life suggests a more negative variation on the basic theme first announced in Sally's story. And so it is with Peter and Bernhard, who in their different way represent a comparable progression from the partially toward the wholly "lost." Peter, the subject along with Otto of "On Reugen Island," is the least interesting of the four characters. Presented far more analytically and undramatically than the others, he is the neurotic intellectual of the 1930's—modeled in part, it would appear, although Isherwood has denied it, on Spender.[6] "More civilised" (88), according to the narrator, who is comparing his selfishness with Otto's, Peter is powerful in will but weak in ego, another of Isherwood's versions of the Truly Weak Man. Unlike Bernhard, who is symbolically and, as it turns out, literally at the end of his road, Peter has only completed part of his journey; and his ugly, impossible, and covertly homosexual relation with Otto is presented as one of the obviously recurrent stages in his unhappy and ineffectual life.

"Peter is only his head" (78); but Bernhard is, as it were, no more than a disembodied ego. Abstaining from the furious activity which, for all its awkwardness, makes Peter somehow Otto's counterpart as well as his opposite and which represents, however futilely, his effort still to make contact with, or even subdue, the world around him, Bernhard is the most isolate and withdrawn of the four. He is long past trying, except for occasional self-defeating "experiments" at connecting with Christopher, to engage himself with others. There are, as Christopher notes when making his first visit to the apartment, "four doors to protect Bernhard from the outer world" (154). Weary, overcivilized, remote, and given, with his habitual detachment, to treating people like children, Bernhard, more than any of the others, experiences a sense of the unreality of his workaday surroundings and even of himself; and it is clear that, when he admits to Christopher that his one belief is "possibly ... in discipline" (160), he is revealing a will, even more powerful than Peter's, not to give in to the void within him.

Bernhard, in fact, in his "arrogant humility" (158), is the completely ironic man, a lonely god so remote from his creation that he can hardly any longer believe in it—or in himself. Unlike the animal-like characters, and despite his position as one of the heads of a large Berlin department store, he is acutely ill at ease with the phenomenal world; he seeks in his typically reductive way some inviolable simplicity—"the negation of a negation" (165) is the narrator's phrase—that will protect him from it. That Christopher sees him repeatedly as Oriental and that Bernhard himself thinks of the East as his spiritual home makes the point symbolically and turns Bernhard into a precursor of those figures of the later novels who are looking more or less consciously for a self beyond the ordinary ego. Bernhard is, however, still of the 1930's, and for him there is no escape except the death he in fact meets at the hands of the Nazis. In that death and in his life generally, one reaches the climax of the book and the end of its steady movement in the direction of isolation, negativity, non-communication, and final withdrawal. By the time one has finished "The Landauers," all of the laughter of "Sally Bowles" has evaporated.

III   Crisis

Goodbye to Berlin ends, however, not with Bernhard but appropriately with another of Christopher's diaries; for what holds together the four characters and their stories is less the interrelations among them, many as these are, than their mutual relation to the narrator, whose potentials or doubles they, like Arthur Norris, are. What Spender said about Isherwood himself, one might say about the narrator, that "so far from being the self-effacing spectator he depicts in his novels, [he is] really the centre of his characters, and neither could they exist without him nor he without them."[7] Of course, Christopher, for all his remarkable fluency, reveals very little directly about himself. The fact is that, as the most complex—and also the most unsettled and chameleonlike—of them all, the one least certain of his own identity, Christopher *cannot* reveal more. And it might be most accurate to say that his friendships, such as they are, are his means to self-understanding, just as they are, more concretely, the reader's means to understanding him.

In the Berlin of the novel, where there is everywhere sham, disparity, and deception and nowhere satisfactory personal relations, Christopher is, in fact, perfectly at home. Giving English lessons to wealthy pupils who refuse to learn or to take him seriously and doing, as far as one can tell, a minimum of writing, for all his dreams of being a novelist, he enters with Sally, Peter, Otto, and Bernhard into relationships that are hardly relationships at all and through them into still more transient encounters with peripheral representatives of The Lost. Corrupted briefly into the life of a hanger-on by Sally's millionaire-lover Clive, vicariously participating through Peter in the stormy liaison with Otto and through Otto in the hysterical household of the Nowaks, Christo-

pher remains essentially the outsider, the confidant of Sally's love
affairs, and, with accurately symbolic appropriateness, the pretended father of her aborted child.

This is not to suggest that Christopher is simply a second rendering of William Bradshaw. Certainly he is less naïve and more
self-aware, and therefore much more easily identified with the
narrator of the book (especially since half of it is in diary form);
but what is more to the point is that Christopher's values seem so
frequently to be the "right" ones, that is, in accord with the author's, that he is as conscious, for the most part, of failures in
others as the reader is. One could demonstrate easily enough that,
verbally at least, Christopher is usually on the side of loyalty, life,
and involvement; his problem is that his values are *theoretical.*
Between his understanding and his ability to act there is, as one
increasingly comes to feel, an unbridgeable gap; for Christopher
is essentially passive, allowing things to happen to him—as when
he finds himself, at Otto's insistence, a boarder in the Nowak
household—or, at most, fighting the good hypothetical fight.

Given the generally "realistic" texture of *Goodbye to Berlin,* it
is the patently symbolic moments, which appear from time to time
in the book, that are particularly revealing of Christopher. The
first occurs as he and Sally watch from Clive's balcony a huge
funeral procession passing below them. Clive's tepid curiosity
about the "big swell" who could have inspired so large a following
provokes in Sally only a yawning reference to the sunset, but in
Christopher, one of his typically ambiguous epiphanies: "In a few
days, I thought, we shall have forfeited all kinship with ninety-
nine per cent. of the population of the world. . . . Perhaps in the
Middle Ages people felt like this, when they believed themselves
to have sold their souls to the Devil. It was a curious, exhilarating,
not unpleasant sensation: but, at the same time, I felt slightly
scared. Yes, I said to myself, I've done it, now. I am lost" (49).

The funeral is that of Hermann Müller, the ineffectual, unin-
spired Chancellor of the Great Coalition; and it is clear that, just
as Müller's futile career mirrors the underlying pathos of Sally's
and Christopher's lives, so their response to his death highlights,
by their disregard of the fact that German democracy is dying,
their failure of involvement in the life of their times.

As is the case with Bernhard, Christopher's lack of involvement
finally calls into question the reality both of the world and of the
self. Thus, when Christopher makes his visit to the sanatorium
where Frau Nowak is an inmate, he has the feeling of being part
of a "rather sinister symbolic dream which I seemed to have been

dreaming throughout the day" (137). Here, in an atmosphere reminiscent of Auden's poem "The Exiles," where "The marginal
grief/ Is source of life" (*Collected Poetry*, 160) or of Paradise Park
in *The Dog Beneath the Skin*, fear and hysteria mingle with a
regressively childish playing at games and at feverish sexuality, in
unconscious parody of the diseased society outside. It is perhaps
some sign of health in Christopher that he is not, like Otto, "very
much at his ease" (133) in this grimly morbid and deathlike world;
but he is enough of it that, when he and the other visitors prepare
to leave the sick, his sense of frightened kinship threatens to overwhelm him (in a vision of being attacked by the patients) as "the
climax of my dream: the instant of nightmare in which it would
end" (139).

Fear in this aggravated and atypically overt form passes, as
Christopher moves from the impoverished Nowaks to the more
respectable Landauers; but there is no change, only a settling of
the mask into place again. In this story, however, there are more
frequent, if still intermittent, eruptions of feeling from the depths:
as when, angry at Bernhard's cousin, Natalia, who has been prod-
ding in her forthright way at his insincerities, he says to her snap-
pishly: "Arguments bore me. . . . The best of all would be for us to
make noises like farmyard animals" (148). The remark and the
situation are even more indicative of Christopher than his visit to
the sanatorium: almost enviably capable of relating on a superficial
level, he has, where genuine feeling is needed, a sense ultimately
only of himself and of his own loneliness. One can therefore say
of him what Pritchett, with less justice, says of Isherwood: "his
characters are tragic, squalid, comical *because* he is cut off from
them. In this respect his compassion is the measure of his fundamental indifference to them."[8]

In any case, it is eminently fitting that *Goodbye to Berlin* should
end, solipsistically, with another diary, and it is very much to the
point that, as compared with the city of the first section, Berlin
here is altogether a more extreme, somber, and dreary place. The
violence, which has been to some degree present throughout the
novel, is now closer to the surface; it increasingly erupts in ugly
scenes of brutality and hysteria: the sickness has become "a kind
of badness, a disease, infecting the world today" (197). The "Diary" itself is grimmer and more explicit in its presentation of the
social, economic, and political scene, more hectic in its movement.
Its chief image is the double vision of the city, which from a
distance glows "so brightly and invitingly in the night sky above
the plains, [but which] is cold and cruel and dead" (187). In its

view of the harsh reality which ironically belies the appearance of warmth and welcome, the description is significant not only for its comment on Germany, of which Berlin is the microcosm, but even more importantly for its allusion to Christopher, between whom and the city a connection is made now, not by symbolic indirection, but by overt comparison. "You seem to belong here" (181), Bernhard tells him at one point; and "A Berlin Diary (Winter 1932–3)" opens with the inevitable identification of its protagonist with the city: "Berlin is a skeleton which aches in the cold: it is my own skeleton aching" (186).

Enough has been said about Christopher to make this analogy plausible, but it remains to be seen how total the identification is meant to be, to what degree the coldness, cruelty, and deadness of the city are his own. In fairness, it should be noted that, in addition to the numerous symbols of death that help to define Christopher and to ally him with his surroundings—not only the structurally important ones like the funeral or the sanatorium but, more randomly, those like the old drug addict, mentioned only once by Christopher in his description of a café he frequents, who "had a nervous tic and kept shaking his head all the time, as if saying to Life: No. No. No" (125)—there are also the opposing, if fewer, symbols of life, such as Christopher's decision, after Sally's abortion, to return to writing his novel. Above all, there is Natalia Landauer, in some ways the most ambiguous character in the novel, and the one who, of them all, may suggest through the pattern of her life a more hopeful future for Christopher.

"The Landauers" opens with Natalia, and most of the first half of the story is devoted to her. From the beginning, there is something odd about her, an incongruous mixture of animation and enthusiasm, on the one hand, and of peremptoriness and stiffness, on the other. As is so often the case in *The Berlin Stories*, one's attention is frequently first caught by the curiously disfigured but expressive English with which Isherwood provides his German-speaking characters and which makes them seem, like Sally when she is mangling German, both touching and vulnerable. But Christopher himself repeatedly points out the more unsettling aspects of Natalia's personality: her tightly held standards, which make her, as he thinks, resemble Bernhard; and above all the almost pathological fastidiousness, which leads her to avoid "all contacts, direct and indirect" (146).[9]

When, after her unfortunate meeting with Sally and the consequent decline of her relationship with Christopher, she apparently vanishes from the novel, it seems more plausible to think of Natalia not only as her cousin's counterpart but, structurally, as a way of introducing his more extreme and complex story. But Natalia does appear once more, a totally different person now; and it seems both significant and typical of Isherwood's work in the 1930's that the change in her should be as much a surprise to the reader as to Christopher and that she herself should appear in her new, redemptive role for only a few of the story's remaining, dreary pages. Short as her appearance is, however, it is clear that she has turned as surely toward life as Bernhard has toward death: her study of art, her love, her imminent journey to Paris, above all, in a book metaphorically ridden with disease, the fact that she is to marry a doctor—all point to *her* salvation at least. "She has escaped—none too soon, perhaps," Christopher thinks after he has seen her at Bernhard's party. "However often the decision may be delayed, all these people are ultimately doomed" (177).

And what then of Christopher? Is his departure from Berlin to be regarded as a comparable escape, as a journey from sickness to health? Certainly, if any of his gestures and actions in the course of the novel suggests a rupture of his identification with the city and what it represents, it is this one. Unlike Fräulein Schroeder, who is already, "like an animal which changes its coat for the winter" (207), adapting herself to the now dominant Nazi regime, Christopher is completely aware of what has happened to Germany. But the final paragraphs of the book, like those of *Lions and Shadows,* throw the whole question of change into doubt. Christopher is taking his last walk in Berlin: "I catch sight of my face in the mirror of a shop, and am shocked to see that I am smiling," he remarks and then goes on to comment, as he observes the apparently ordinary scene around him, on its "striking resemblance to something one remembers as normal and pleasant in the past—like a very good photograph. No. Even now I can't altogether believe that any of this has really happened ... (207)." The by-now familiar images of smiling and of the mirror are revealing and so too is the incredulous, the emotionally short-circuited, response to the events that have occurred. But the reference to the photograph is the most telling, bringing us back as it does to the beginning of the first "Diary" and to the mechanical, uncreative, implications of the narrator's statement: "Some day, all this will have to be developed, carefully printed, fixed" (1).

The image of the camera reintroduces and reinforces the theme of disengagement; and it becomes clear that, if Christopher is a different person from William Bradshaw, the dissimilarity has to do not with any change that occurs to him in the course of *Good-bye to Berlin* but with what he is as it opens. It is possible, certainly, to view the novel in linear terms, as the progressive exploration of the temporal degeneration of Germany, or better still to see it, in accordance with Isherwood's notion of a "dynamic portrait," as opening out and expanding (although here the reference is rather to the reader's understanding than to the protagonist's growth). But its underlying pattern is finally that of a circle: events change, but Christopher does not; for Berlin there is the negative resolution of disaster; for Christopher, the temporary expedient of more traveling. Yet insofar as Christopher and Berlin are symbolically connected in the novel, it can be assumed that, if there is no visible alteration in him, there is nonetheless a mounting intensification of stress on his inner and generally hidden life, one articulated indirectly in the sequence of characters from Sally to Bernhard.

Goodbye to Berlin moves, then, not, as *Mr. Norris* and *Lions and Shadows* do, to self-awareness but rather—at that point where the increasingly oppressive line of characters and events intersects the circle of repetition and frustration evident in Christopher—to a state of crisis. For Isherwood's contemporaries, the presentation of this crisis was in itself the justification and achievement of the novel. So John Lehmann described it in the year of its publication "as one of the few successful solutions in recent years of the problem of reconciling the claims of the artist and the claims of the moralist who is aware of, and passionately rejects social injustice and social decay, and sees what forces are arising in the pattern of history to challenge them. The *implication* of Christopher Isherwood's work is entirely revolutionary, humanist in the most active sense of the word, though he is never *explicitly* propagandist."[10]

For a reader of today, armed with the wisdom of hindsight, *Goodbye to Berlin* is also the final stage of Isherwood's early work. Before the appearance of his next novel, Isherwood had left England, settled in America, and made his conversion to Vedanta. His protagonist, traveling as always more slowly than Isherwood himself, is to be found in that novel still in England and still in crisis but ready at least and able to formulate and express, if not yet to solve, the problem he inherits from his prewar predecessors: *Goodbye to Berlin* is good-by to the 1930's as well.

CHAPTER 6

The Divided Generation

WHILE WRITING *Lions and Shadows* and *The Berlin Stories*, Isherwood was also collaborating with Auden on three plays and a travel book, which, as much and perhaps more than his fiction, helped to establish his reputation at the time and to make him one of the period's representative figures.[1] Understandably, the long prose "Travel-Diary" of *Journey to a War* (1939)—since it is, in its final form at least, completely Isherwood's work[2]—most closely resembles the novels. The plays, on the other hand, particularly the first and the third, represent a new phase in Isherwood's work. In their aggressive tone and spirit, in their stress on the need for active commitment, they come far closer to the kind of writing Virginia Woolf criticized in her essay, "The Leaning Tower," and to what Spender had in mind when he said of himself and his contemporaries in the 1930's: "We were divided between our literary vocation and an urge to save the world from Fascism."[3] Isherwood's novels stand as probably the most successful fusion of private integrity with public morality in the decade; the plays and, to a lesser degree, *Journey to a War* are among the many shots fired in its long propaganda war against "The Enemy."

I The Plays

With some exceptions, it is difficult to determine Isherwood's exact share in the composition of the three dramas.[4] He has referred repeatedly to his own role as that of Auden's librettist,[5] "working only on the plotting and part of the prose" (*Exhumations*, 5). Joseph Warren Beach has conjectured, plausibly, that "Isherwood was evidently more interested in the satirical and comic modes in propagandist drama, whereas Auden wished to emphasize the moral and affirmative elements in their social faith."[6] But, in the plays as they stand, the two strains are not ultimately separable: the ferocious and sometimes funny attacks on the "old gang" entail a faith in "the army of the other side" (*Dog*, 108); and it is assumed, not always with any obvious justification, that destruction will lead to a new and better life. Ideologi-

78

cally, then, if not technically, the plays are as much Isherwood's as Auden's. For both writers, if for Isherwood in particular, the public medium of the theater appears to have provided release from a more habitual restraint and to have afforded the opportunity to accomplish what the protagonists of the novels successively fail to do—to engage themselves in and become part of some corporate spirit larger than the narrow confines of the self.

Anger and affirmation are especially marked in *The Dog Beneath the Skin* (1935) and *On the Frontier* (1938). In both, irony, which in the novels is an instrument of discrimination, a vehicle for examining the complexities of human behavior, is transformed instead into the tool of a single-minded satirical purpose. In the plays, as a consequence, the tentative moral implication of the fiction either becomes tendentious or deliquesces into the unearned and sentimental assurance of revolutionary fervor. In dramatic terms, the ironic and sentimental aspects of the two plays are rendered in a total opposition between the forces and manifestations of the Establishment on one side and the all-embracing concept of love on the other: in the absence of love, it is implied, lies the cause of society's pervasive sickness; in its rediscovery, the hope for "another country/ Where grace may grow outward and be given praise" (*Dog*, 112).

The heroes of the plays—if one can use the word for Alan, who, as Spender has aptly phrased it, "is a Candide with the mental age of Peter Pan,"[7] or for Eric and Anna, who are stiff and wooden caricatures of romantic lovers—serve largely to expose the evils of their world; but to a degree they also embody and thereby particularize them. In *The Dog Beneath the Skin*, Alan, traveling in search of the long-lost Francis, is obviously on one of the false journeys that recur in Auden's poetry. Against the background of the various corruptions in church and state that are to be found in all the countries he visits, there is enacted, sketchily, the drama of his own fall into the perverse forms of love, suggested first in the Red Light District of Ostnia, with its "magical acts of identification" (34), then in the escapist atmosphere of Paradise Park, and finally in Alan's symbolically narcissistic affair with a shop-window dummy. His disenchantment and Francis's renunciation of the dog's skin he has been wearing are the prelude to a long Mortmere-like speech by Francis, filled with armies, enemies, fighting, and battlefields, and to a final exhortation from the chorus to love to enter the real world and conquer among the sterile. It is, obviously, a call to the already converted, stirring in its way but hardly subject to analysis. What lies behind its optimis-

tic faith and its sometimes shrill rhetoric is the facile belief that in
the many the one will both lose and find itself, emerging whole
but no longer alone.

The Dog Beneath the Skin, despite its perfunctory and episodic
construction and its precipitous plunge into wish fulfillment, is the
best of the three plays, thanks to its humor, its speed, and Auden's
remarkable poetry. *On the Frontier* is more prosaic in its demand
for commitment and also more schematic in its analysis of the
causes for the war that breaks out in the course of the play, a
nationalistic, capitalistic war that blinds the workers to the true
class struggle. Part of the trouble with the play is that its villain is
so much more vivid than its pallid hero. Valerian, the ruthless,
power-seeking financier, a potential variant of the ironic man, is,
paradoxically, the most humanly admirable of the characters. Perhaps because he can or does feel so little, there is a quality of
bravery and even nobility about him that is given full play in the
otherwise silly scene of his death. He is limited, certainly, by the
crude irony that is directed at him and at everything he stands for,
but not so much as Eric is by being his authors' puppet and
mouthpiece. Eric's shift from pacifism and personal relations to a
recognition that "we must kill and suffer and know why" (119) is
justified by the play's theoretical substructure but hardly by its
dramatic movement.

In general, *On the Frontier* is even more extreme and certainly
less convincing than *The Dog Beneath the Skin* in its presentation
of life as it is and as it will be. What is palpable in the play is the
savage dissection of the neurotic leaders and their lonely, hysterical followers; the title itself supplies the main metaphor for the
present—the boundary line that isolates and separates countries,
lovers, workers from one another and that encloses individuals
within themselves. By contrast, the future, with its vision of a
world freed from restraint, remains, however much insisted upon,
a shadowy hope: the ending of the war by the soldiers and the
fraternizing of the former enemies takes place off stage;[8] the
meetings of Eric and Anna are accomplished only by way of fantasy; and the lovers' final predictions about "the lucky guarded
future" (120) appear in the context of a windy and improbable
Liebestod.

But the penultimate section of the play, an interlude in which
the readers of five different newspapers contradict each other's
reports of the war, does most to undermine and call into doubt the
sanguine expectations that Eric and Anna express before their
death. John Lehmann describes an earlier version, in which "a

revolutionary end followed the outbreak of war between the two states, the people seizing power. In the final version," he goes on, " ... frustration is briefly substituted for the original 'straight' solution, producing an effect of bathos after the steadily increasing dramatic tension of what has preceded it."[9]

The fact that another ending was also written for *The Dog Beneath the Skin*—in this one Francis is murdered, and the journalists announce: "Nothing has happened"[10]—suggests that Auden and Isherwood were at times themselves in doubt about the final directions of their plays. It is therefore of some importance in interpreting both the dramas and the attitudes of the two men between 1935 and 1938 to note that the revisions of the first and last play suggest, respectively, a movement toward a more and a less hopeful conclusion. And, in fact, the latter play, for all its perfervid enthusiasm, its hortatory call to the workers of the world, who, as many critics have pointed out, were hardly in a position to understand the words being addressed to them,[11] is hollow and sentimental, a forced attempt to believe in what by 1939 Auden was referring to as "a low dishonest decade" (*Collected Poetry*, 57).

The beginnings of disillusion are, however, present in the earlier play as well, not only as a function of the social situation but as a part of man's personal and ontological nature. As in Auden's other poetry and Isherwood's novels, there is in *The Dog Beneath the Skin*, by way of a persistent undertone, a sense of time passing and death impending, of the terrors of consciousness, of "Man divided always and restless always" (97). Except in the play's assumption that the more specifically psychological ills are related to the state of society, it shirks confrontation with the ineluctable horrors of life and living that it so convincingly presents; and these appear again, more insistently, in *The Ascent of F 6* (1936), the most bitter of the three plays.

F 6 is in fact two plays, although considerable ingenuity is expended in trying to make them cohere. One deals, like *The Dog Beneath the Skin* and *On the Frontier*, although in a more rigorously psychological fashion, with the false forms, here the "involuntary privation" (117), of love and the consequent perversions of the will into an agent of destruction and self-destruction. The other, which is both more interesting and less clearly articulated, is concerned with the will as the instrument and guarantee of the ego's reality, the faculty not simply of right choice but of action generally. The first, by implication at least, views as possible the end of error; the second necessarily calls into question all objects, good as well as bad, to which the will is attached. Michael Ransom is the play's hero not only because he is capable, belatedly, of self-knowledge but also because his desire to be honest makes him susceptible, as his twin brother James is not, to that *taedium vitae* which is his most difficult challenge.

Late in the play, James is revealed to be "The Dragon," of whom Auden writes in one of his poems:

> When a man sees the future without hope,
>   Whenever he endorses Hobbes' report
>   'The life of man is nasty, brutish, short',
>   The dragon rises from his garden border
>   And promises to set up law and order.[12]

As the leading representative of the militant, nationalistically competitive, and conservative ruling class of England and as the unmoving mover of the precipitous climb to the top of the mountain, James opposes patriotism and adventure to the boredom, the incompleteness, and the anguish of existence that haunt Mr. and Mrs. A, the painfully average choric figures of the play, who are its most obvious victims of the dailyness of life. But for the A's there are at least, through their vicarious participation in the more exciting, public actions of the drama engineered by James, occasional, unstable moments of fulfillment and the sense that life may after all have meaning.

For Michael, however, as the leader of the doomed expedition, there is only the increasingly painful awareness of his motives and of the unreality of his life. Ostensibly his brother's opposite, he is in fact his double: both are types of Isherwood's "Truly Weak Man." But Michael alone undertakes "The Test," only to learn that he is as flawed and corrupted in his private life as James is in his public actions. On its most obvious level, the play moves relentlessly to the exposure of Michael's Oedipal jealousy of James as the source of his pride and his desire for power. His death—despite the chorus' assurance that his mother, James, and the others who have in some way been responsible for it are among those "Whom history has deserted" and who "to dissolution go" (183)—is pathetic rather than redemptive; and the play ends with an ironically fragmented gabble of voices shouting for honor, sacrifice, and duty. In this sense, *F 6* is not, like the other plays, a call to commitment but a gloomy exploration of the nature of and the reasons for commitment. Michael Ransom, Isherwood has said, was modeled on T. E. Lawrence (*Exhumations*, 13);[13] but the historical value of the play comes from its relevance to the 1930's in general and in particular to Auden and Isherwood themselves. *The Ascent of F 6* does, or tries to do, a good many things; it is tempting to think that it is, *inter alia,* an attempt at self-analysis.

In any case, the real climax of the play comes not in the all too obvious revelations about Michael's psyche but in his confrontation with the Abbot of the monastery. It is here, prior to the final climb, that he recognizes his need to save mankind; and it is also here that the Abbot delivers what *may* be, whether or not it was so intended, the central speech of the play: "You know, as I do, that Life is evil. You have conquered the first temptation of the Demon, which is to blind Man to his existence. But that victory exposes you to a second and infinitely more dangerous temptation; the temptation of pity; the temptation to overcome the Demon by will" (153).

Despite the fact that the Demon or, at any rate, Michael's Demon is later shown to be his mother, the Abbot's words appear to transcend the narrowly psychological formulation the play invites by its ending. When, after echoing James's abiding faith that "as long as the world endures there must be order, there must be government," he goes on to say, "but woe to the governors" and to recommend "The complete abnegation of the will" (154), he strikes a note to which something not only in the plays but in Isherwood's novels vibrates—a covert dissatisfaction that was to become manifest only later in Isherwood's conversion to Vedanta. At the same time, there is an obvious danger of reading backward into the play. Isherwood has described the scene with the Abbot as "all flummox, rubbish";[14] and, in the confused and confusing context of *F 6*, it is difficult to determine whether the Abbot is only one of the play's extremes or its ideological center.

Michael continues his climb, praying, "Save us, save us from the destructive element of our will, for all we do is evil" (155); and he falls victim to more malignant forces than either he or the play can overcome. The Abbot's message, then, remains ambiguous, another sign, as Spender noted in his general criticism of the plays, of "an acceptance of rather facile compromises whenever the plays demanded a real fusion of Auden's fantasy with Isherwood's ironic realism."[15]

II   *Journey to a War*

Perhaps because its point of view is first person and its form that of a diary or because it is the least collaborative of the works we have been discussing, the "Travel-Diary" that occupies some three-quarters of *Journey to a War* is a less simply propagandistic work than the plays. Not that there is any mistaking the bias of the book or its commitment to the Chinese cause, but direct statements are few and its partisanship is generally implied. In this sense, the "Travel-Diary" falls somewhere between Isherwood's novels and his plays: less strident in tone or revolutionary in emphasis than the latter, it is, even though its focus is frequently blurred, more openly dedicated to a cause than the longer fictional works.

Its intention, predicted in the dedication of the book to E. M. Forster, is best summed up in the feelings about war attributed by Isherwood to Auden but obviously concurred in by him as well: "War is bombing an already disused arsenal, missing it and killing a few old women. ... War is waiting for days with nothing to do; shouting down a dead telephone; going without sleep, or sex, or a wash. War is untidy, inefficient, obscure, and largely a matter of chance" (202). Given this belief and attitude, the "Travel-Diary" aims, through its habitual understatement, its studied avoidance of the melodramatic or even the dramatic, at an antiheroic presentation of the *human* reality of war.

This is not to suggest that the "Travel-Diary" is a dingy chronicle of squalor and suffering. Forsterian in texture as well as in attitude, it manages, without evading the ugliness and terrors of war, to articulate its simultaneous response to the Sino-Japanese conflict and to a confused, suffering, transnational humanity in a voice that is most often comic and, at its most successful, ironic, somewhat in the manner of the novels, particularly of *Lions and Shadows*. The techniques are familiar enough: the dry, tea-tabled descriptions of ruin and desolation; the jokes that seem necessary and even brave in the midst of discomfort and danger; the deflating juxtapositions of theoretical principle with a more ambiguous reality. Irony, then, operates in different ways in the "Travel-Diary": sometimes to complicate the easy assumptions of wartime mentality; at others, to heighten the reader's response to the appearances of war, making the horrific more horrifying still.

There is, however, one irony obviously not, or not fully, intended by the "Travel-Diary" since its effect is finally to undermine and even subvert the book's intention. As in the novels, the problem revolves around the nature and the characteristic vision of the first-person narrator. Indeed, as one reads "Escales"—an account, published separately, of the Auden-Isherwood trip from Port Saïd to Hong Kong—and then the opening pages of the "Travel-Diary," one has a sense of *déjà vu:* apparently one has come again upon William or Christopher, off on another journey, this time as the self-conscious and ineffectual tourist-reporter not quite adequate to the war he has stumbled into. Here, in "Escales," is the disease imagery so familiar from *The Berlin Stories*;[16] here, at the beginning of Isherwood's section of *Journey to a War*, the excited spectator, and then the "neutral observer," feeling, like Christopher at the end of "The Nowaks," that everything is "dream-like, unreal" (28); here, also, a few pages on, the narrator's struggle to enter emotionally into what, cognitively, he recognizes as real. And Isherwood continues to present himself from time to time as the confused or uninvolved onlooker, now nervous and fearful in contrast to Auden,—"the truly strong" (75) man, possessed of "monumental calm" (120)—now embarrassed by his money and position and filled with guilt, as he allows himself to be carried by sweating coolies. In short, he is, as in the picture Isherwood presents on the last page of the "Travel-Diary" "the well-meaning tourist, the liberal and humanitarian intellectual, [who] can only wring his hands over all this and exclaim: 'Oh dear, things are so awful here—so complicated. One doesn't know where to start'" (253).

About *this* figure there is no problem: the narrative voice so far described—although, relatively speaking, more aware and more engaged than those of the protagonists of the novels—is still, with obvious intention, limited and undermined by Isherwood's irony. The disparaging self-portrait is, in fact, an oblique affirmation of the need for involvement. But there is another and more prominent voice in the "Travel-Diary," different not in what it says but in that its words are not, as far as one can determine, qualified by Isherwood's moral disapproval. The first voice is subject to authorial control, but the second *is* the author's, less isolable but even more influential, through its constant presence, in determining the final effect of the work. It is, in short, in the latter case, as if William Bradshaw and the creator of *Mr. Norris* were in fact the same person. The ultimate ironic quality of the diary, then, has to do not, or not primarily, with a disparity between author and narrator but with that between two contradictory visions run together indiscriminately and with no apparent sense of their incongruity.

Fundamentally, what is at issue here is a question of perspective: habituated by the opening pages of the "Travel-Diary" to looking both through and at the narrator, the reader finds himself suddenly reduced to single vision. The landscape is the same, but his guide has become in truth the reporter he before only pretended to be. What had been, and sporadically continues to be, a purposeful underplaying of anger and commitment is now an absence of those qualities, so that the general technique of the "Travel-Diary" is increasingly at odds with the moral emphasis generated by certain particular, local effects.

What is it, then, that determines the quality of the diary's second, unmediated voice? In part, certainly, responsibility lies with the levelness of Isherwood's tone: the intelligent, controlled, moderately distant interest that tends to remain the same throughout, whether describing an air raid, a Chinese opera, a military briefing, or an interview with high officials; in part, with his characterization of the slightly schoolboyish, gamelike relationship with Auden, which so often usurps the foreground of the action; and especially with his all too obvious penchant for seizing upon the comedy of any situation. In short, one has too often the uncomfortable feeling that the humanness of war is being swamped by a more general sense of human absurdity; the response to the immediate situation is continuously diluted with a string of anecdotes for which the miseries of the Chinese supply only one, and that not the most important, of the sources. In the final analysis, *Journey to a War* is not really about a war but about a visit to a country that happens to be at war. Witty, interesting, and lively, it is not, although it is obviously meant to be, moving, as Orwell's less well written *Homage to Catalonia* is. Like the plays, the "Travel-Diary" suffers from internal inconsistency; but where they fail through an excess of badly motivated sentiment, it fails through an insufficiency of feeling. In the contention of the two voices, it is the second that wins out, the tourist at the last who takes precedence over China.

It is one thing to describe the failure of a book; another, to account for it. It has been suggested already that, under the pressures of collaboration, Isherwood revealed more openly and less well than in the novels that the problems that dog his protagonists from 1928 to 1939—the growing disillusion, the urgent need and the frustrating inability to make a commitment, the increasing sense of division between self and world—are his own. *An Approach to Vedanta* (1963), a short autobiographical sketch, which includes an account of these years, lends some substance to these speculations. It reveals, retrospectively, the less conscious tensions within Isherwood, manifested at the time in the inability to "stop traveling" and in his having "become constitutionally restless" (6), which led in 1939 to his realization not only that he was but that he "had always been a pacifist" (6).

It is, then, the final irony in this chapter of many ironies that, as a result of his fullest involvement in the public life of his own times, Isherwood discovered what his plays and travel book, in their ambiguities and contradictions, had already revealed—that he was looking for something quite different from the "New Country" of the 1930's. Or perhaps it is the next-to-final irony. "During the mid-thirties," Isherwood writes in *Exhumations*, "I would have described myself as an atheist, a liberal, a supporter of the Popular Front and an advocate of armed resistance to fascism, in Spain and everywhere else" (97), and it is this image, derived in large part from the works written with Auden, that was used against him when, in January, 1939, he left England for America.

Having done so, Isherwood ceased to be, for the time at least, "a hope of English fiction."[17] He became instead, along with Auden, the object of an angry and outraged protest against what was taken to be a selfish desertion both of their own principles and of England in the critical months prior to the outbreak of war. "What I don't see," announces one of the characters in Evelyn Waugh's *Put Out More Flags* (1942), where Auden and Isherwood appear as the poets Parsnip and Pimpernell, "is how these two can claim to be *contemporary* if they run away from the biggest event in contemporary history."[18] But Isherwood, already a pacifist, was soon to become a Vedantist, thereby establishing for himself an altogether different relation to contemporary history or to history of any kind.

Appropriately enough, Isherwood's work in the 1930's opens with a translation of the *Journaux Intimes* of Baudelaire, whom he was later to describe as "one of the first writers of 'the poetry of departure'" (*Exhumations*, 28); and it ends with an atypically parabolic story, "I Am Waiting," about a sixty-seven-year-old bachelor, a mild uninvolved failure at life, who awaits the fulfillment of a preternatural experience. "Perhaps I shan't survive the journey," he writes. "But I wouldn't refuse to make it, on that account, even if I could. What other experience can be comparable to this? What else have I to live for now? So let the moment call for me when it will—at whatever time, in whatever place. I shall be ready" (*Exhumations*, 230).

Even if one tries to guard against the temptation of making "I Am Waiting" into a thinly disguised allegory of Isherwood's inner life, it is difficult not to sense in the story *his* readiness as well— a readiness, after the failure of the 1930's, for a commitment of a different kind. This Vedanta supplied; and the second half of

Isherwood's career, remarkably similar though it is in its preoccupations to the prewar novels, shows everywhere the difference in perspective. For the travelers of Isherwood's writings in the 1930's, life is a journey without a map: behind the world of human obligations there is the shadow of human frustration; behind it, the familiar twentieth-century void. The protagonists of the later works exist, whether or not they know it, *sub specie aeternitatis.*

PART II *THE GOD WITHIN*

CHAPTER *7*

Toward The Still Point

C OMING TO *Prater Violet* from Isherwood's novels of the
1930's, one has, at least until the last ten pages of the book, the
sense of retracing familiar ground. The scene of the book is England; the period, which follows immediately upon the events in
Goodbye to Berlin, 1933–35; the narrator and protagonist, once
again Christopher Isherwood, involved now, with the Austrian
director, Friedrich Bergmann, in the making of a film, but burdened still with the weight of his persistent, insoluble problems.
At one point in the novel, Bergmann says to Christopher: "The
film is a symphony. Each movement is written in a certain key.
There is a note which has to be chosen and struck immediately.
It is characteristic of the whole" (50). Considering the cinematic
quality of *Prater Violet*, one finds in Bergmann's statement the key
to the novel as well: the opening words, almost immediately repeated, are Christopher's name.

Indeed, the major themes of the entire novel are predicted in
its first scene: if the reiteration of the protagonist's name—it soon
becomes Kreestoffer Ischervood and then Mr. Usherwood—signals the usual problem of identity, then the comically frustrating
efforts to bring about a meeting between him and Bergmann point
no less surely to the difficulties of communication. Forced again
and again in his confused telephone conversations to say, in effect, "I am I," Christopher finally lapses into German in a last,
desperate effort to make himself understood.

At the same time, there are in these early pages the even more
important glimpses of Christopher's home life: he, acting the part
of the sophisticated and blasé writer to the appreciative audience
of his family; his mother, a more sweet and subtle version of the
Demon figure of Isherwood's and Auden's prewar writings, in-
dulging and controlling his performance. "You are a typical mother's son," Bergmann tells him. "It is the English tragedy. ... It is
a disaster. It will lead to the destruction of Europe" (42).

I   Problems of Technique

If, however, Christopher is as absorbed as his predecessors in the complexities and problems of the self, and in very much the same way, Isherwood's own approach is a very different one: both more explicit in announcing its themes and more conventionally symbolic in its articulation of them; more immediate in its effect and more discursive as well, a type of shorthand statement that threatens at times to subordinate the dramatic tensions of the book to the schematic pattern imposed upon it.

Thus the film that provides the novel with its main action and with its title is the vehicle for at least four different and easily separable comments on the characters and their responses to the events of the period. Most obviously, "Prater Violet," with its factitious and sentimental plot, is meant to contrast with the horrible reality of contemporary Vienna under Dollfuss; and, in the opposition of art and life, make-believe and actuality, there is generated the clearest of the book's ironies. At the same time, Bergmann's willfully distorted twisting of the plot into an account of "the dilemma of the would-be revolutionary writer or artist, all over Europe" (71) supplies a complementary evaluation of the situation of the modern intellectual, that divided figure who "from the safety and comfort of his home ... permits himself the luxury of a romantic interest in the proletariat" (72) and who "wants to crawl back into the economic safety of the womb. He hates the paternal, revolutionary tradition, which reminds him of his duty as its son" (74).

The connection between the private and the public is familiar enough in the early novels, especially in *Mr. Norris*, but the point is made differently here. Forced for the moment to substitute Bergmann's allegorical reading of the film for his own ironic response, the reader is likely to feel that he is being, however relevant the accusation of Christopher may be, too cleverly manipulated by Isherwood himself to accept the indictment as a valid comment, certainly his most overt, on the failure of his whole generation. It is only one step more to recognize in Bergmann's prediction Isherwood's own retrospection and to lose, in the awareness of its historical relevance, a sense of the novel's fictional immediacy.

The other interpretations of the film "Prater Violet" depend on the nature not of its content but of its form. In this sense, the film takes on the larger meanings, first, of the creative process (as contrasted with the more limited created object) and then of life itself. As Bergmann's artistic achievement lies in his effort to transcend his unworthy materials, so his personal achievement lies in his response to the conditions of human existence. For Bergmann, to live is to be a prisoner; to create, to commit a crime; to encounter the world, to undertake a Dantesque journey through Hell.[1] And, as these images recur in the novel, involving the more passive Christopher as well, it becomes clear that life, as envisaged in *Prater Violet*, is a horrible comedy through which people move, playing their parts, sharing a common plight as captives of a Kafkaesque universe, where, as Bergmann says, "They torture us, and we have nothing to confess" (94), but unable for the most part to make contact with one another.

Sharing the view of existence as symbolic drama, Isherwood treats his characters very much like the events and objects of the book. He limits them, for the most part, to strictly functional roles and makes them representative figures, symbolic of sharply divergent attitudes to the novel's personal and political themes. Thus the elegant, gentlemanly Ashmeade; the malicious, insensitive journalist Patterson; and Lawrence Dwight, the exponent of art for the sake of order, represent in different ways—the respectable, the egocentric, and the esthetic—paradigms of English disinterest in and ignorance of the Austrian situation and its implications for England. Even Bergmann, whose values are meant to be sufficiently significant and inclusive to give the lie to the three men and to Christopher as well—indeed, to the English in general—enters *Prater Violet* as a symbol: "the face of a political situation, an epoch. The face of Central Europe" (23).

With Bergmann, Isherwood's characterization receives its most difficult challenge. Intended obviously, apart from Christopher, as the novel's most complex figure, the Austrian must not only justify in himself the norms of the book but must lead the reader, through the resonance of his personality, to see in the superficiality and flatness of the others a failure of character and of perception, as well as a justification for Isherwood's mode of presenting them. Isherwood's method, particularly in the earlier sections of the novel, is to work for depth in his portrait by superimposing onto the outline-sketch of the creative exile layer upon layer of analogical description: Bergmann is by turns Aesop, Punch, a Roman emperor, a tragicomic clown, a Jewish Socrates. And, in his snorting, growling, groaning, and grunting, he is also meant to suggest a more passionate, uncontrolled quality within himself. But in *Prater Violet* the effect of applying animal metaphors to a character has less wholeness and integrity than in the earlier novels: the same images no longer have the same value in Isherwood's rhetoric; and Bergmann, who in his gloomier way is very much in the line of Forster's Mr. Emerson, remains less human than a type of humanity, decorated with a variety of attributes intended to reveal his complexity and fallibility. In short, Bergmann at the end, as at the beginning, of the novel, is a symbol of redemption, and he is Isherwood's first major attempt to humanize a saint instead of, in his more usual manner, making a sinner charming.

If Bergmann is less interesting than what one takes Isherwood's conception of him to have been, the failure is to be found not simply in the realization of a single character, however important, but, more radically, in the setting forth of the relationships among characters and in the nature of the stylistic context the novel provides for them. What is ultimately lacking in most of *Prater Violet* is a sense of tension. Characters are not simply symbolic; they are isolated in their symbolic roles. If part of the novel's intention is to convey this isolation, it remains nonetheless true that Isherwood's technique overreaches itself in becoming less a medium for than an imitation of his vision: action gives way in large part to dialogue and dialogue to speeches, so that the implications of the earlier novels here become statements, for which the characters are only too transparently the vehicle.

Furthermore, much of what is wrong with the book has to do with Christopher's role in it. One would expect to find in the economy of *Prater Violet* some figure capable of providing a sense of dramatic interaction with the stormy director, since the Ashmeades and Dwights are so patently strawmen to be bowled over by Bergmann; and Christopher, because he is the novel's narrator and protagonist and because he is Bergmann's ironic counterpart, presents himself as the obvious choice. He is, however, and clearly with intention, made less prominent and less central to his book than his predecessors to theirs.

In 1943, Isherwood wrote to John Lehmann about his work on *Prater Violet*: "I'll have to find a new *tone of voice* because the ventriloquist has changed somehow, and needs a new dummy."[2] The new tone of voice emerges in *Prater Violet* from a character who, although or perhaps because he is more humanly responsive than the earlier protagonists, more knowledgeable as well as more explicit about his problems, is in effect less absorbing than they. With less to wonder and speculate about, the reader is more easily able to place and dismiss Christopher than the theoretically more neutral and cameralike narrators of *The Berlin Stories*. In a recent interview, Isherwood explained "that because Bergmann is such a dominating character it doesn't matter that the observer is kept down, is not allowed to emerge. I think a great and amusing feature of the book is that right at the very end you discover that Christopher had a life of his own which he never even mentioned to Bergmann."[3] But, of course, it does matter: to suppress the narrator through nine-tenths of the novel and then reveal in a rush the contours of his inner life is to run the risk, when one realizes what has happened, of calling attention primarily to the cleverness of the author.

Furthermore, in making Christopher not ironically but flatly an observer, Isherwood exposes the reader, since Christopher *is* the book's narrator, to the drabness of his prose. If Cyril Connolly's remarks about Isherwood's style[4] apply to any of his books, then it is, after the fact of the criticism, to *Prater Violet.* The following passage provides a typical example: "The year was drawing to an end. The newspapers were full of optimism. Things were looking up; this Christmas was to be the greatest ever. Hitler talked only of peace. The Disarmament Conference had broken down. The British Government didn't want isolation; equally, it didn't want to promise military aid to France. When people planned their next summer's holiday in Europe, they remembered to add, 'If Europe's still there.' It was like the superstition of touching wood"(79). The resemblance to Isherwood's prewar style is clear enough, but the earlier manner has here become almost a mannerism. Still simpler in diction—there are, except in Bergmann's speeches, far fewer images—and made up of more short, simple sentences, Isherwood's style retains its speed and "readability" but lacks edge. Flatter as well as sparer, it remains ironic in form but not in function: given the vision and character of the narrator, the tight, syntactically discontinuous sentences create in the paragraph as a whole not a series of significant gaps but of obstructive potholes. One progresses through the verbal landscape with a sense of slightly strained and weary movement, as if riding repeatedly over the same broken road.

II Problems of Perspective

With the last section of the novel, however, there is a change.[5] Differing in almost every way from what has gone before, these pages constitute a kind of epilogue to the novel; and in the contrast between them and the rest one finds the principal source of irony in *Prater Violet.* Whereas in the earlier novels, because of their style and point of view, irony is experienced as the simultaneous perception of disparate meanings, here narrative technique, with its appropriately cinematic use of montage and rapid cutting, renders irony primarily a function of the novel's linear construction and makes one's awareness of the book's incongruous elements both more explicit and more a temporal experience.

Continuity is provided between the two parts of *Prater Violet* by a more emphatic restatement in the second section of certain of the novel's images and themes. Once again Christopher is "a traveler, a wanderer" (178); life, a journey where people meet and pass like actors coming together briefly on stage during the performance. Once again, the problems of communication and identity are central. Paradoxically, it is "that hour of the night at which man's ego almost sleeps" (178), and it is also that time when Christopher feels most burdened by the awareness of himself as an oppressively separate entity. For the last section of the novel belongs to the narrator: adopting suddenly a more intense, a more somberly analytic tone, he begins to lay bare the unstable foundations on which he has been building his life. And he reveals in the process the state of modern man as described by Alan Watts in his book on Vedanta: "In the act of putting everything at a distance so as to describe and control it, we have orphaned ourselves both from the surrounding world and from our own bodies—leaving 'I' as a dis*content*ed and alienated spook, anxious, guilty, unrelated, and alone."[6]

Christopher's experience, then, comes as the culmination of what all his predecessors in Isherwood's novels have felt. He is the ironic man *in extremis*, aware, with his remote, if hardly detached sensibility, of the absurdity of his world and of himself, certain only that the "I" which is his definition is also his prison. Inevitably, he comes, or Isherwood brings him, to that point at which Camus begins his essay on the absurd: "Il n'y a qu'un problème philosophique vraiment sérieux: c'est le suicide."[7] "What makes you go on living?" Christopher speculates, and his personal answer comes as a testimony to his characteristically obsessive bondage to the ordinary, a bondage conceived not as a principle of life but as a mere habit, an inevitable *pis aller* in a senseless universe: "I supposed, vaguely, that it was a kind of balance, a complex of tensions. You did whatever was next on the list. A meal to be eaten. Chapter eleven to be written. The telephone rings. You go off somewhere in a taxi. There is one's job. There are amusements. There are people. There are books. There are things to be bought in shops. There is always something new. There has to be. Otherwise the balance would be upset, the tension would break" (179).

The key not only to Christopher's state of mind in this last section but to the technique that reveals it lies in the phrases "a kind of balance, a complex of tensions." The style, no longer monotonous, generates excitement through a merging of opposed effects. On the one hand, there is a greater syntactical variety and frequently, as in the paragraph just quoted, a reduction of the simple sentences which help to create the texture of the rest of the novel to mere phrases and sentence fragments. On the other hand, the writing becomes generally more descriptive, more imaged, and even more rhetorical, as in the use of anaphora throughout these pages. Paratactic in its disconnected simplicity, unwontedly rich in its artifice, the style embodies the contrast between the ironic and sentimental modes that constitutes the dialectic of Christopher's mind in his agitated confrontation with himself.

Christopher differs from the earlier narrators, then, both in the intensity of his dissatisfaction and, more significantly, in his ability at least to imagine ways of overcoming those obstacles to some interpersonal or transpersonal union that is the goal of almost all twentieth-century literary characters from Yeats's speaker in "Among School Children" to Albee's lonely twin in *The American Dream.* This desire for communication, for destroying barriers, and even more radically for merging the self with something other than the self, which I have called "sentimentality," takes a variety of forms in the epilogue to *Prater Violet,* where the need for union fights its difficult ideological and emotional battle against the protagonist's habitual sense of separateness and fear.

What is most interesting to observe in these various alternatives to his lonely and paralyzed state that, more or less consciously, Christopher entertains in turn, is the progress or at least the movement which they describe from the personal to the impersonal. Each solution points more emphatically than the last to the final and inevitable dissolution of the self—the goal, as the reader is made to see, of all Christopher's futile efforts to integrate the divisions within himself. As his thoughts turn first to love, one immediately senses in him an ambivalent straining toward and away from the possibility of relationship. Almost caught up by the sentimental picture he paints for himself of the vacation he is to take with "J.," his current lover, he begins shortly to undercut the romance still to come by anticipating with ironic circumstantiality not only the end of the affair but also the succession of lovers to follow. Ineluctably, "it would be wonderful" (180) entails, even, or perhaps especially, in the realm of fantasy, "We would part" (181).

It soon becomes apparent that, for Christopher, lovers are "only

trophies, hung up in the museums of each other's vanity" (181);
loving, a "box of tricks" (181); love, however romantically conceived, a matter of sex; and sex, "the need to get back into the
dark, into the bed, into the warm naked embrace, where J. is no
more J. than K., L., or M. . . . And the end of all love-making, the
dreamless sleep after the orgasm, which is like death" (182). What
is at issue here is not, as one might suspect from the use of initials
for names and from the studied avoidance of revealing personal
pronouns, that the love is homosexual but that it is infantile, narcissistic, and egocentric; that it is built on the shifting sands of an
ego seeking, not to realize itself in the mutuality of a relationship
with another, but to escape (futilely, as the subsequent, apocalyp-
tic vision of war, fear, and "Death universal" [182] demonstrates)
from itself into oblivion.

The reference to "the private fears of childhood" (182) makes,
almost too obviously, the connection between Christopher's Oedipal obsession and his frustrated attempts to find security in his
quasi-anonymous lovers or in the act of sex itself. By contrast, the
final communication with Bergmann, which brings to its climax
the novel's main relationship—the meeting, as the imagery explicitly indicates, of father and son—suggests a turning toward
maturity, responsibility, and manhood: "the paternal, revolutionary
tradition." Indeed, in this momentary, symbolic connection of the
would-be artist with the genuine creator one hears the single,
redeeming note in the book.

If *Lions and Shadows* is Isherwood's *Portrait, Prater Violet* is his
Ulysses, with Christopher playing Stephen's role of negative, uninvolved intellectual and Bergmann, the exiled Jew, suggesting
Bloom's abundant and earthy humanity. Like *Ulysses, Prater Violet*
is in some sense a novelist's novel, playing off against and sometimes submerging its hero in its own technical experiments; and
one can understand why, in the light of its *conceptual* brilliance,
it is, as Isherwood has indicated, one of his books that satisfies him
most.[8] What makes plausible the comparison between Joyce's massive work and Isherwood's far less complex one, however, is the
similarity of their underlying patterns: the crossing in a moment of
time and through some inexplicable law of moral dynamics of the
paths of two radically dissimilar men; the redemption—hypothetical, ambiguous, still to be proved—of the younger; and, finally,
their parting.

But if the ultimate contact of Bloom and Stephen is mysterious
and transcends words, that between Christopher and Bergmann
takes place still farther below the level of daily personality:

"Beneath outer consciousness, two other beings, anonymous, impersonal, without labels, had met and recognized each other, and had clasped hands" (184–85). What seems at first to be suggested is one of those intuitive encounters that justify the often painful personal relations in the novels of Forster and Woolf, but there is more to the meeting than that. If the most that Christopher can achieve is this transitory clasping of hands, it is not the most that Isherwood offers him. Beyond and underlying human relationships, as Christopher's words suggest, there is something more fundamental that exists outside of the categories of "I" and "you" and that makes final union possible, because it is common to and the same in all men. *Prater Violet* has no Molly Bloom; what it offers instead as its final vision—now not as sexual escape but as positive fulfillment—is the loss of the self.

For Christopher, however, the thought of transvaluing his life offers itself at the moment as a possibility more frightening than desirable. "I see something else," he thinks, after meditating on his fear: "the way that leads to safety. To where there is no fear, no loneliness, no need of J., K., L., or M. . . . 'No,' I think, 'I could never do it. Rather the fear I know, the loneliness I know. . . . For to take the other way would mean that I should lose myself. I should no longer be a person. I should no longer be Christopher Isherwood' " (183–84). What Christopher perceives, momentarily and incompletely, in this passage which so ironically echoes the confident assertion of his name on the first page of the book, relates, of course, to the substance of Isherwood's recently acquired Vedantic beliefs. The question is how the reader is to judge Christopher's rejection of that truth about himself and his existence which henceforth provides, in one form or another, the philosophical background of each of Isherwood's novels.

The answer is partly ambiguous and ironic in Isherwood's familiar manner. After the epilogue, *Prater Violet* returns abruptly for its last page and a half to a defensively casual tone and to something very much like the earlier style. Moving away again from the protagonist and his self-examinations, the final section suggests a parodic coda to the book as a whole, a tidying-up, in a tea-tabled version of nineteenth-century novel endings, of leftovers. The narrator's brisk comments record with amused impersonality the later history of the film and note the various reactions to it of different viewers. Thus, one is inclined to see in Christopher, after his transitory illumination, a regression back to his earlier state. But remembering the encounter with Bergmann that ends the epilogue—a pledge, it would seem, of his eventually coming to terms with the truth that lies at the heart of *Prater Violet*—one is tempted to see as well in the seemingly random references to his mother, to Lawrence Dwight, and finally to Bergmann, with which the narrator allows the book to trail off, a symbolic charting of the movement of his own life. From the cosy and infantile attachments of his home to an inhuman concern with art, he moves at the last to genuine creation and concern. If this is the case, then Christopher, however far behind his creator, is at least moving in his direction; and *Prater Violet* may be viewed, despite the tentativeness and incompleteness of its protagonist's progress, as the most affirmative of Isherwood's novels so far.

CHAPTER 8

Ego and Atman: A Note on Vedanta

I SHERWOOD HAS himself so often and so lucidly set forth the basic tenets of Vedanta[1] that it would be at the least supererogatory to explain them again in detail. A short, synoptic view of his beliefs should, however, make clear their relevance to *Prater Violet* and to the novels that follow it. Fundamentally, truth for Isherwood in the postwar phase of his career inheres in the belief that "we have two selves—an apparent, outer self and an invisible, inner self. The apparent self claims to be an individual and as such, other than all other individuals. . . . The real self is unchanging and immortal. . . . Our real nature is to be one with life, with consciousness, with everything else in the universe. The fact of oneness is the real situation. Supposed individuality, separateness and division are merely illusion and ignorance" (*Vedanta*, 19–20).

What becomes immediately apparent is the degree to which Vedanta accommodates, even while it reshapes, Isherwood's prewar concerns. Here again is the ego, obstinate in its will to survive, no less potent for being seen in some ultimate sense as unreal; and here also, the desire for transcendence, now conceived, not in terms of social commitment, but of religious awakening. The struggle between personal identity and otherness persists; and it is significant, in the light of Christopher's inchoate strivings in *Prater Violet*, that Yoga, as Isherwood explains, in *An Approach to Vedanta* "means, basically, 'union' " (*Vedanta*, 19). Union had been and now continues to be the goal of all Isherwood's protagonists and, it seems safe to say, of Isherwood himself.

But to observe the basic continuity of Isherwood's thought and temperament is not to question the validity of his religious experience. A psychologically reductive approach is especially easy when dealing with the phenomenon of conversion; but the etiology of a belief, it need hardly be said, is not the test of its truth. Isherwood himself has been candid enough in suggesting causes for his turn to Vedanta—notably, his dissatisfaction with himself and his life in 1939 and the attraction, to an inveterate opponent of authority, of a non-dualistic creed, "a practical mysticism, a do-it-yourself religion which was experimental and empirical" (*Vedanta*, 23). All of this is, however, in a sense beside the point; the decision of how far to credit the claims of Vedanta in the abstract is one for the individual reader; its effective use in the novels is another matter.

The influence of Vedanta on Isherwood's later writings has to do both with the nature of his vision and the shape of his books. *Prater Violet*, for all its obvious links with the books that precede it, marks the beginning of a reorientation in Isherwood's career, most apparent in the transformation of the romantic and relativistic irony of the early novels into the transcendental irony of the later ones or, in Northrop Frye's terms, in the inevitable movement of fiction from irony to myth.[2] But the change, as *Prater Violet* and as Isherwood's relatively small output of novels between 1945 and 1962 suggest,[3] was not necessarily an easy one. At their best, the later novels, deriving as they do from a comprehensive and coherent system of beliefs and values, convey simultaneously and with equal dramatic validity Isherwood's continuing preoccupation with human action and motives and with his new metaphysical assumptions—a double vision of man seen through his own eyes and, as it were, through those of God. Where the later works fail, they reveal, in contrast to the lack of sufficient focus that sometimes obscures the early ones, an overly theoretical structuring of experience. If the prewar novels seek above all to *discover* value, the postwar books attempt rather to demonstrate the *consequences* of belief.

But not in a doctrinaire way. "He sought, surely," Spender wrote of Isherwood's conversion, "a novelist's philosophy; for the novelist, least of all artists, can afford to be a dogmatic moralizer."[4] In fact, Isherwood's moral sympathies broaden as his thought becomes more teleological; his tolerance, contained now within a metaphysical framework, derives from a sense of communion not, as in the 1930's, with "The Lost," but with all human beings following their many paths to the truth.

As a consequence, Isherwood's eye continues to focus, as Huxley's after his turn to religion did not, on the humanness of human beings. There is no immediate and dramatic change in the protagonists of the books; enlarged though their sense of themselves and their problems gradually becomes, their significance and interest remain functions of their personal and interpersonal struggles. What changes is Isherwood himself; writing for the first time with a moral assurance substantively different from that of his characters, he is seeking an adequate formal and, particularly, a stylistic equivalent for the new ideology by which they are now judged. If his experiments are, as *Prater Violet* is, sometimes strained and self-conscious, the problem is in a sense that of all religious novelists who are faced with the need to translate the ineffable into esthetically comprehensible terms. *Prater Violet,* the first fruits of Isherwood's conversion, is in length and conception the least adventurous of his efforts to resolve the problem—a matter, perhaps, of *reculer pour mieux sauter;* but the novels that follow explore in increasingly greater depth the relation between the known and the unknown.

In any case, what Isherwood asks of the reader is not a detailed knowledge of an exotic religion but a general comprehension of what Huxley has called "The Perennial Philosophy"—the few beliefs common to all mystical religions. Thus Vedanta, where it is artistically assimilated into the texture of the novels, is no more intrusive, although more coherent, than the moralities of the earlier works; and in supplying Isherwood with a more stable vantage point from which to observe his human actors, his religious beliefs make possible in the postwar novels a greater variety of characters and relationships and a broader sense of perspective in dealing with his familiar problems.

In one way, however, the later books show little or no change. Observing the diverse forms of affection, friendship, fascination, common interest, and fraternal feeling in them, one misses still, with one notable and curious exception,[5] any evidence of love: the mature, mutual responsiveness of independent adults. Whether one regards Vedanta as cause or effect of this ultimate failure of human communication, whether one sees it as a solution to or a continuing evasion of Isherwood's problem in the 1930's, the fact remains that these novels take as their ideal not relation but fusion. So Christopher recognizes Bergmann, with some lack of consistency, both as his spiritual father and as a fellow being who, like his own authentic self, is "anonymous, impersonal, without labels." Commitment, except through the mediation of the Atman, the common God-substance in all men, remains incomplete, abortive, or transitory. Isherwood's new faith makes human action potentially more purposive but hardly more rewarding in and of itself; the center of the universe remains the "I," now searching not for mundane involvement but for its final rest.

CHAPTER *9*

Progress of a Soul

T HE WORLD IN THE EVENING (1954) is the first of Isherwood's predominantly religious novels. As compared with *Prater Violet*, in which the brief and tentative suggestions of "that other way," "the way that leads to safety" (183), are conveyed through a largely self-imitative technique, this novel represents a thoroughgoing attempt to explore fictionally the now dominant concerns of Isherwood's personal experience and to discover a different formal means of expressing them. That the attempt fails does not diminish the value or interest of the book as an introduction to the more complex novels that have since appeared; but, considered in itself, *The World in the Evening* is the least successful of Isherwood's works. In part, Isherwood's difficulty in accommodating spiritual truth to the novel is a conceptual one; but the inadequacies of the book are explicable largely and more satisfactorily in technical terms: *The World in the Evening* undoubtedly expresses Isherwood's need to engage himself more completely with his new subject; it expresses, however, more clearly still and somewhat negatively the desire to leave behind the esthetic strategies he had evolved during the 1930's.

I Form and Meaning

Something of Isherwood's intention as he prepared to begin his book in 1947 can be found in a letter to John Lehmann: "At all costs," he wrote, "I'm resolved not to be funny. . . . People resent being amused more than anything, I've decided."[1] That Isherwood accomplished what he set out to do is clear enough—*The World in the Evening* is his most humorless novel—but it is difficult to applaud the change in view of the results. The shift in tone, which Isherwood describes in his letter, inevitably entails an alteration in the *nature* of moral statement (quite apart from the question of its content); and it is therefore not strange that his most solemn book is also his most tendentious.

There is, furthermore, a connection between the moralistic obviousness of *The World in the Evening* and the rigidity of its structure. As compared with the parodic form of *Mr. Norris*, or with the ironic appearance of formlessness in *Goodbye to Berlin*, the design of Isherwood's postwar novel is curiously stiff and theoretical. At the same time and still more destructively, the overelaborated structure—with its clues and hints, its slow revelations, its multiple perspectives and time shifts—fails to overcome the prevailing sense of randomness that so frequently threatens to overwhelm the pattern of the novel, as the seeming randomness of *The Berlin Stories* never does.

Isherwood uses form, then, in *The World in the Evening* not to articulate but to support and enclose meaning; but the meaning thus enclosed constitutes only part of Isherwood's total vision. The radical disjunction between the realistic and symbolic modes of the novel is the clearest indication of Isherwood's inability to integrate the opposing spheres through which many of his characters and in particular his protagonist, Stephen Monk, move. The nature of the opposition is intimated by the lines from which the title of the novel is taken:

> I sing the progress of a deathless soul
> Whom Fate, which God made, but doth not control,
> Plac'd in most shapes; . . .
> . . . .
> And the great world to his aged evening;
> From infant morn, through manly noon I draw.[2]

Since the discovery of or the failure to discover the "deathless soul" is the subject of all Isherwood's later novels, *The World in the Evening* is typical of them in its concern, on the one hand, with the world of time—with its oppressive sense of individual identities, of isolation, of inadequate communication—and, on the other, with the world of the spirit. The characters of the prewar fiction live exclusively in the dimension of time, the world of the ego, as Isherwood came to regard it after (and, more intuitively, even before) his conversion; those of the later novels are presented at least with the possibility of choosing eternity, the world of the Atman or, in the present novel, of the Inner Light.[3] But, if *The World in the Evening* differs from the earlier novels in its intimations of immortality, it contrasts no less significantly with the ones that follow it in its conception of how the human and the spiritual are related: the dissimilarity between *The World in the Evening* and Isherwood's novels of the 1920's and 1930's is an indication of its

ambitiousness; its dissimilarity from those of the 1960's indicates, instead, its lack of success.

The position of the novel in the sequence of Isherwood's writings is, however, less anomalous than transitional. The point can
most cogently be made by considering the novel in terms of those
transformations in the nature and function of irony that take place
in Isherwood's career as a whole. In this perspective, the earlier
novels may be said to exhibit an "irony of limitation," in that the
extent and even the quality of change envisaged in them is such
as to leave intact Isherwood's basic conception of existence as
temporally limited and without ultimate significance. To be sure,
these novels repeatedly expose the failures of their protagonists to
act upon, sometimes even to understand, the moral values that are
central to Isherwood's thought at the time. But detached *or* involved, William, Christopher, and the others are restricted to the
state of "being in time," which, as Northrop Frye has recently
written, is the basis of the ironic vision.[4] As we saw earlier, the
growing sense of dissatisfaction that appears in the novels through
Goodbye to Berlin belongs not only to their protagonists but to
Isherwood himself, so that, whatever the differences between
them that make irony possible, the affinities are substantive and
strong.

In short, Isherwood in the 1920's and 1930's can see further but
not much further than his characters: sharing with them a humanistic and fundamentally relativistic morality, he is capable of en-
visaging the improvement but not finally the transformation of
temporal existence. Even in these early novels irony is an instrument of many uses, exploring, correcting, and at the last despair-
ing of what it reveals; and its most curious function is that, for lack
of an alternative, it reinforces, even as it exposes the limitations of
the world it depicts.

By contrast, Isherwood's three most recent novels suggest the
terms "irony of liberation" and "irony of reconciliation." The first
phrase refers obviously enough to the fact that the characters of
the postwar novels, however comparable in their initial predica-
ments to those of their predecessors, are offered, hypothetically at
least and as a result of their attitudes and actions, the possibility
of final release from the world of time. That few manage to transcend their egos and that fewer still even come near to discovering that deeper self which is for Isherwood freedom and
liberation is in itself irrelevant to the vision these books present.
The most substantial change in the later novels is not in what the
characters do but in the cosmos they inhabit, not in what they

learn but in what Isherwood knows. Inevitably, then, since what is only potential in these characters is actualized as a sustaining belief in Isherwood, the relation between him and them, as well as the quality of irony with which he treats them, is far different from that in the earlier books. Based as it is now on an essentialist view of truth, Isherwood's irony is both more distant from and more compassionate in its attitude toward existential reality; and, if the temporal remains for the most part the more interesting of Isherwood's two worlds, it is because it continues to be for him, in Keats's phrase, "the vale of Soul-making."

This last point is an important one. Certainly Isherwood's irony in his novels of the 1960's acts to reveal the disparity between the world of time and the world of spirit and also to judge the former in terms of the latter as ultimately less real. But human action remains for Isherwood of value and interest in itself and, especially, in its consequences. Salvation, in Isherwood's view, is effected in time not in eternity, so that to deny completely the human sphere is to negate as well the very possibility of redemption, particularly since the loss of the self is regarded as both a difficult and a gradual process that is attained completely only by a very few. For these reasons, the ironic vision of the last novels aims not, certainly, to equalize but to reconcile time and spirit— or, to put it another way, to trace in the former the progress of the soul. One can say, then, that the ironic vision of the earlier novels becomes in the 1960's only one term in a more comprehensive attitude, whose basic belief is the unity of all things. In *The World in the Evening*, however—in effect, if not by intention—Isherwood demonstrates the differences but not the relation between his two worlds; and the result is that the book testifies to the very fact of separateness which it means theoretically to deny.

II   The Dynamics of Change

The most successful parts of the novel are those that reveal dramatically the psychology of Stephen Monk, the least attractive and most thoroughgoing of Isherwood's egoists. Certainly Stephen bears a marked family resemblance to a number of Isherwood's earlier protagonists; but, as his capacity for self-deception is larger and his characteristic sins of omission more serious, so his empathetic imagination is proportionately smaller. Quoting Shakespeare's sonnet, "They that have power to hurt and will do none,"[5] Stephen's first wife, Elizabeth Rydal, accurately defines the ugliness and corruption of that technical innocence which is her husband's legalistic defense against moral obligation. Refusing

to recognize Elizabeth's terrified awareness of her approaching
death, and cultivating toward his importunate lover, Michael
Drummond, an attitude of playful detachment, Stephen typically
seeks from the world at large the unearned response that he needs
to keep his image of himself intact.

The tarnishing of that image is the progressive work of the three
relationships which provide the focus of Stephen's adult life. His
marriage to a woman twelve years older than himself clearly
represents a transposition into a more complex key of *Prater Violet*'s concern with "the dream of the mother," and various responses during his life with Elizabeth—notably his jealousy of his
unborn child and his relief at its death—emphasize his need to
maintain his role. His inability to do so becomes obvious in his
attempt to re-create after Elizabeth's death the relationship with
Jane Armstrong, whose apparent independence of and indifference to him threaten his persistent need to assert his identity at
the expense of others and bring him to an awareness—felt, if not
yet understood—of the unsubstantiality of his existence. "What
you need, Steve," Jane tells him in an unconsciously grim parody
of his first marriage, "is a mother or a nurse" (254); and her own
marriage to him completes the cycle in this more explicitly pathological vein. But Jane is, after all, only an instrument in what is, at
the deepest level, an act of *self*-destruction. For however much
Stephen apparently desires to affirm his selfhood, the more fundamental drive of his being is revealed in his need to lose the self
—a need that is first, and more convincingly, the symbol of his
desire for escape and finally the key to his salvation.

In his earlier affair with Michael Drummond, Stephen's covert
fantasy of freedom from responsibility is most interestingly formulated. Superficially, the relationship suggests that, like the un-
moved mover of the Shakespearean sonnet Elizabeth quotes to
him, Stephen is again asserting his mastery. Furthermore, the fact
that Stephen enters into a homosexual relationship with someone
described by his first wife as "our eldest son" (153) appears to
indicate a reversal of his usual dependent role. But Stephen's first
sexual encounter with Michael reveals what is in fact the truth: his
deepest satisfaction is in his release from maturity and in his
movement toward, first, the mirror-world of narcissism and then,
still more regressively, the liberating indiscriminateness of the in-
fant's polymorphous world: "in the darkness I remembered the
adolescent, half-angry pleasures of wrestling with boys at school.
And then, later, there was a going even further back . . . wanting
only the warmness of anybody" (194). Inevitably recalling Chris-

topher's meditations on love at the end of *Prater Violet*, the passage defines not only the quality of Stephen's relationship but also and more fundamentally the need finally to be annihilated, to participate through the merging of anonymous bodies in the extinction of the self.

In any case, Stephen finally comes against the appropriately shoddy background of the evening world of Los Angeles, to a recognition of the futility and sterility of his life; and Isherwood is without question at his best in reducing his protagonist to this point—in showing how, within his limited psychological range, Stephen moves retrogressively toward a greater and greater degree of egocentricity, until his mingled involvement and disgust with himself render him incapable of even the most perverse and self-regarding kind of love. But it is typical of *The World in the Evening*, and of the technical flaws noted in it, that Isherwood feels compelled to substantiate his analysis by superimposing on it a repetitive and static verbal pattern of references to Stephen's immaturity and irresponsibility, the effect of which is to create, misleadingly, an image of Stephen himself as unchanging and thus to subvert the more subtle delineation of him in his interactions with others.

Stephen as unregenerate egoist is a part of the novel's past, revealed by his later self through a series of flashbacks. In the novel's present, Stephen ceases to convince, and here too one become aware of Isherwood's more general problems with characterization. The characters who pass in and out of Stephen's sickroom play, not much more convincingly than Stephen himself, a double role in the book: first, as realistic figures independently responsive to their own complex worlds of war, concentration camps, homosexuality, creativity, and charitable works; and, second, as heuristic symbols demonstrating or revealing to Stephen the truth he eventually comes to recognize. To say that in their former capacity they effectively engage the reader's curiosity is only partly to praise Isherwood's skill in conceiving them, since the interest that these characters generate for the book as a whole works in fact to destroy its cohesion.

The pattern of *The World in the Evening*, as the titles of its individual sections all too schematically indicate, concerns Stephen's development from selfishness to selflessness; and in this movement the other characters have their place, but only as fragments of their richer selves. For the rest, the realistic details of their lives mount up without accumulating organic significance, while the failure to resolve them into the restrictive pattern of the

book causes the symbolic actions and statements of the characters
to obtrude. Redundant in the presentation of Stephen's egoism,
symbolism in the rest of the novel is simply unrelated to the un-
redeemed world of time in which Stephen and the others move
more naturally, if without supernal grace.

Among these characters, Elizabeth, as a figure from the past,
presents a somewhat special case. As she appears in her husband's
memories, Elizabeth seems to bear some responsibility for the difficulties of their relationship; revealed in her letters, however, she
is a very different woman—almost, in fact, a saint. As one tries to
adjust the two perspectives, it becomes clear that Isherwood's
portrait achieves not complexity but inconsistency; and it is hardly
surprising that he has subsequently acknowledged "something
phony about her"[6] or that he has expressed the wish that he "had
desanctified her more."[7] Following the by now familiar pattern,
Elizabeth sacrifices human density for symbolic clarity; and there
is at any rate nothing problematic about what she is meant to
illustrate in her letters. This attitude Isherwood describes in his
Vedantic writings as "nonattachment," the ability to perform an
action sacramentally, without either fear or desire.[8] To make this
point, Isherwood devotes a large part of the novel to Elizabeth as
writer and to the problem of her reputation; and, in portraying the
continuous erosion of the latter throughout the novel, Isherwood
clearly means to affirm the primacy of Elizabeth's integrity and of
her honesty to her talent.[9]

But Isherwood's concern is not simply with the ethics of
creativity. In *An Approach to Vedanta,* he maintains that
"theoretically at least ... *every* action ... may be a stepping stone
to spiritual growth, *if* it is done in the spirit of nonattachment"
(*Vedanta,* 61).[10] And, in confirmation of Isherwood's statement,
Elizabeth—dying, struggling against her elemental animal fear,
her deeply rooted sense of separateness, and her need for her
husband—achieves the awareness for which the whole of her life
—or, more accurately, her career—is the preparation. This revelation is also Isherwood's central belief: "I'm sure now (I used not
to be) that there's a source of life within me—and that It can't be
destroyed. ... I, like everything else, am much more essentially in
It than in I" (236).

Although Elizabeth is more articulate than the other figures who
surround Stephen during his convalescence, still she is paradigmatic both as a character and as a vehicle of truth. Others in *The
World in the Evening* also come, if less consciously, to some
awareness of "It," not necessarily in Elizabeth's terms but at least

as a force realized through relationship and activity. So Stephen's "Aunt" Sarah, despite some attempt to suggest limitations in her and in the "wonderfully horribly drearily wholesome" (21) Quakerism she represents,[11] functions in the novel primarily as another embodiment of spiritual reality. Indeed, as a picture of practical and affectionate busyness, Sarah comes even closer than the intellectual Elizabeth to the un-self-conscious and somewhat cloying goodness that is, for the moment, Isherwood's ideal. And what is true of Sarah is also true of Stephen's other friends; they too, in their obvious symbolic roles, present Stephen with the concrete example—the same example—of involvement and commitment achieved through sacrifice and in spite of personal loss.

Returning to Stephen, one may say that the presence of so many teachers implies a singularly inapt pupil. The redemptive role filled by Bergmann in *Prater Violet* is now divided among some half-dozen characters, as if the reader were to regard the collective weight of their example as an inevitable spur to Stephen's improvement and the sheer quantity of their faith and devotion as a sign of his inner grace. It is, in any case, both suspect and disconcerting that Isherwood provides a virtual chorus of testimonials to Stephen's likelihood of success. One after another, Gerda, Charles, Sarah, Jane, and even Stephen himself express their certainty that he will emerge a better person in the future. But it is significant that none of them is able to say why he feels as he does, only, like Sarah, that he is "quite, quite sure" (292). The insistence on both the certainty and the ineffability of this knowledge makes of Sarah and the others so many good fairies at the birth, or in this case the rebirth, of the traditional prince; and Stephen's own comment on the change he feels in himself—"It's a sort of miracle" (267)—only confirms the reader's suspicion that he is being offered magic as a substitue for motivation.

Isherwood is not so facile as to suggest that Stephen is at the end of his spiritual journey, but clearly he is meant to be much further along the way than Christopher is at the end of *Prater Violet.* The muted and ironic resolutions of the earlier novel are here replaced by an explicitness of affirmation that seems to indicate not so much certainty as the desire for it. With a ruthless tidiness the novel contrives in its final section to disentangle and sweep away all of Stephen's problems: just as his new, more objective and more tolerant attitude toward his father, his foster mother Sarah, and his pseudo-mother Elizabeth represents a liberation from the past and a new equilibrium in the present, so his enlistment in a civilian ambulance unit predicts a future of concern for and involvement with others. None of Isherwood's earlier protagonists manages to leave so far behind the limiting world of the self.

The central problem of *The World in the Evening,* however, is neither what Stephen is as the book opens nor what he has become by its close; it is how Isherwood effects the transition from one to the other—how he articulates the dynamics of change. Again the intention is clear enough: Stephen is obviously meant to undergo, in the second and longest section of the novel, something in the nature of therapy or exorcism, in which the healing agents are Elizabeth's letters and the more substantial presence of his visitors. But not all of Isherwood's rhetorical strategies—the rooting of Stephen's rites of passage in a mass of circumstantial detail; the use of a narrator who expresses so much more overtly than his predecessors his sense of frustration and dissatisfaction with himself; and the manipulation of the novel's time scheme so that one becomes acquainted only gradually with the worst there is to know about Stephen—overcomes the reader's skepticism: *The World in the Evening* remains the most obviously "constructed" of Isherwood's novels. And when, presumably to make Stephen's capacity for growth more credible, Isherwood provides him with the ego-denying experience of "total, instantaneous awareness" (94), one is bound to ask how the Stephen who until this stage of his life is scarcely capable of recognizing the independent existence of others is suddenly able to attain, in however sporadic and momentary a fashion, to glimpses of "absolute otherness" (17).

The answer, it becomes increasingly apparent, is that in one of its aspects at least *The World in the Evening* is less a novel than a fable of redemption; and if one fails to recognize in the fairy-tale hero off to war the quite different Stephen who returns to his childhood home, it is because there exists between the two a difference that is conceptual rather than, as in some of the earlier novels, temporal and because the operative principle of the book is not growth but metamorphosis. The passivity to which Stephen is literally reduced through most of the book suggests, in fact, only the limited possibilities of growth open to the first-person narrators of the earlier novels. As an inhabitant of the world of spirit, Stephen is an interloper, admitted with the aid of false credentials. So Isherwood, asked by an interviewer whether he intended anything specifically religious in Stephen's progress, answered vaguely but suggestively: "Well, perhaps that's the whole trouble. Maybe it should have been much more or much less than it was."[12] The "much less" points backward to the limited, temporal worlds of Christopher and William, and the "much more" gestures toward Isherwood's novels of the 1960's, in which, abandoning or at least modifying his effort to encompass Stephen's two roles in one character, he achieves both the dramatic conflict and the ironic reconciliation that his transitional novel lacks.

The World in the Evening is in some sense a cautious book, operating still, despite its religious concerns, within ordinary moral terms. With *Down There on a Visit*, Isherwood moves toward a morality of extremes. Stephen, however, for all the harm he does, remains one version of Isherwood's *homme moyen sensuel*. Insufficiently good to attain a conventional heaven, insufficiently bad to become a modern saint, he is extreme in his reward but not in his character. *Down There on a Visit* transforms the banality of evil into the evil of halfheartedness; in the development of his new ethic, *The World in the Evening* represents only an apprentice work.

CHAPTER 10

The Road of Excess

D OWN THERE ON A VISIT (1962) records the final appearance of Isherwood's most ubiquitous protagonist, and one's awareness of witnessing the end of a fictional partnership of almost thirty years undoubtedly helps to give the book its distinctively valedictory quality.[1] There are, however, more substantial reasons for viewing the novel in this way: covering the period from 1928 to 1953, *Down There on a Visit* contrives to suggest within the framework of its four stories the material of most of the earlier books—sometimes by alluding directly to their events, more often by implying their presence in the intervals among the stories— and thus provides a synoptic view of Christopher's and, *mutatis mutandis,* of Isherwood's life and career.

Furthermore, the narrator's concern in *Down There on a Visit,* as in the other books in which the protagonists bear Isherwood's name, is in a general sense an investigation of the self and particularly of the conditions of his own selfhood. Once again, and even more insistently, Christopher poses to himself the familiar questions: Who am I? What does it mean to be I? Once again his typical situation is beginning a trip; his characteristic gesture, looking into a mirror. Once more, finally, the search for identity is carried on obliquely and not always with Christopher's full comprehension by the exploration of a series of characters who represent his symbolic potentials.

Down There on a Visit marks as well a return to humor. Or perhaps, after the tonal experiments of *Prater Violet* and the calculated drabness of *The World in the Evening,* it is more accurate to describe a progression toward a new kind of comedy, both exuberant and controlled, in which Isherwood's moral concerns manifest themselves through the medium of what is described in *The World in the Evening* as "Quaker Camp" (111). "You're expressing what's basically serious to you," Stephen's friend Charles tells him in that novel, "in terms of fun and artifice and elegance" (110). Like *The Berlin Stories* and *Lions and Shadows, Down There on a Visit* achieves a combination of matter and manner that

is at once ironically suitable to the character and to the perceptions of its protagonist and esthetically congruous with the greater
comprehension of its narrator.

But the book differs precisely in that Isherwood and, to a somewhat lesser degree, his narrator display an understanding, based
on the assurance of belief in Vedanta, that goes beyond anything
of which either William Bradshaw or the earlier Christophers are
capable. There is the usual danger of confusing Isherwood with
his narrator: Christopher even in his final phase remains, in terms
of the novel's religious and ethical norms, insufficiently responsive
to what he recognizes to be right. But his understanding of and
belief in Isherwood's values make him at least a more reliable
surrogate for his creator than any of his predecessors. So, at the
very beginning of the novel, he reveals his recognition of both the
discontinuities and the resemblances among his various selves and
thereby establishes the temporal perspective from which they are
to be viewed: "We have in common the label of our name, and a
continuity of consciousness; there has been no break in the sequence of daily statements that I am I. But *what* I am has refash-
ioned itself throughout the days and years, until now almost all
that remains constant is the mere awareness of being conscious"
(14).

Under the influence of that awareness Christopher begins his
Proustian reconstruction of the past, and, although he employs,
successfully for the most part, a whole range of devices—notably
diaries and present-tense narration—to suggest that he has, as he
puts it, "shut down my own foresight" (16), one remains conscious
throughout of his relatively confident and comfortable presence,
revealing itself in the characteristic style of the novel. Coming
after the stylistic impoverishment of *Prater Violet*, the self-con-
sciously bright and clever flatness of "Take It or Leave It,"[2] and
the uneconomical and imprecise laxness of *The World in the Evening;* coming before the more sophisticated experiments of *A Single Man* and *A Meeting by the River, Down There on a Visit*
exhibits what may be thought of as the median, if not quite the
typical style of Isherwood's later period.[3] It therefore deserves
comparison with *Lions and Shadows*, the book which the later
novel most closely approximates in stylistic qualities, as it does
Goodbye to Berlin in narrative technique.

The following passage, so reminiscent of a number of paragraphs quoted in the first chapter of this study in its spatial perspective and in its visual and auditory movement toward
attenuation and remoteness, provides a good starting point: "The

shot crashed out, startlingly violent in that quiet place, and back volleyed the echo from the sheer cliffs of the shore—against which the waves rose and spread themselves and withdrew, rose and spread and withdrew, like an opening and withdrawing hand. A distant sheep dog began barking frantically from somewhere behind the grove. Other dogs answered him, very faintly, high up on the mountainside" (81). As in *Lions and Shadows,* one is immediately aware of the different kinds of grammatical sentences, of the proliferating form of the first and longest sentence, and of the mixture of concrete and generalized elements in the diction. But equally apparent, both verbally and syntactically, is the fact that the passage conveys a richness and fullness of poetic suggestion largely foreign to the earlier book. In the inversion of the second member of the first sentence ("back volleyed the echo"), in the subdued but persistent alliteration throughout, and particularly in the repetitive and cadenced formation of the last half of the opening sentence, one perceives a relaxation of Isherwood's earlier and more abrupt manner in a way that parallels the change, described earlier, in the structure of his ironic vision.

It would be misleading, however, to take a single quotation as an absolute pattern for Isherwood's writing in *Down There on a Visit.* One of his major successes in the novel lies indeed in the fact that, among its four parts, he creates a stylistic and tonal variety appropriate to the various characters who predominate in each and achieved largely through the high proportion of dialogue and diary entries in the book. So the distinctive quality of "Waldemar" is determined by Christopher's exacerbated nervousness, anger, and fear in the immediate prewar period and by the corresponding rhetorical inflation of the style with a profusion of questions and exclamation points. The style of "Paul" is conditioned by Augustus Parr's fantastic images and tropes and by Paul's own colorful, vigorous American speech. Nonetheless, it is possible to detect in the novel as a whole, beneath surface differences in texture, some fundamental stylistic constants.

The opening paragraph of the book helps to suggest what these are and to point up in particular the sense of cohesiveness that contrasts with the characteristic discontinuity of *Lions and Shadows* and that accounts for the central difference between Isherwood's early and late styles:

Now, at last, I'm ready to write about Mr. Lancaster. For years I have been meaning to, but only rather halfheartedly; I never felt I could quite do him justice. Now I see what my mistake was; I always used to think of him as an isolated character. Taken alone, he is less than himself. To present him entirely, I realize I must show how our meeting was the start of a new chapter in my life, indeed a whole series of chapters. And I must go on to describe some of the characters in those chapters. They are all, with one exception, strangers to Mr. Lancaster. (If he could have known what was to become of Waldemar, he would have cast him forth from the office in horror.) If he could ever have met Ambrose, or Geoffrey, or Maria, or Paul —but no, my imagination fails! And yet, through me, all these people are involved with each other, however much they might have hated to think so. And so they are all going to have to share the insult of each other's presence in this book. (12)

As compared, for example, with the opening of *Goodbye to Berlin*, these lines are, thematically, remarkable enough in their focus not on the egocentric isolation of Christopher from the world around him but on the interrelatedness between him and the people with whom he is to come into contact. The evidence of a controlling awareness is, therefore, however ironically presented, apparent from the beginning. Stylistically, the contrast with *Goodbye to Berlin* is even more striking: in place of the abrupt, subjectless fragments that introduce Isherwood's novel of the 1930's and establish the disjunctions of that world, one is offered a series of measured and balanced sentences, building up rather than down for their effect and creating the sense not of a mind in the process of thinking but of an intelligence already aware of its direction. Above all, one recognizes the new prominence in Isherwood's prose of conjunctions which cement the various parts of the paragraph so as to leave none of the intervals that are the distinguishing feature of Isherwood's prewar style. If division is the ineluctable fact of the earlier novels, joining is the desired goal of the later ones; and the underlying belief in the possibility of union manifests itself stylistically throughout *Down There on a Visit,* even when the narrator withdraws his presence in order to present more directly to the reader's view the confusions and uncertainties of his younger selves.

I   "Mr. Lancaster"

The passage just quoted illustrates as well that explicitness of statement which, though less troublesome than in *The World in the Evening,* is nonetheless found in *Down There on a Visit,* particularly in the first of its stories, "Mr. Lancaster." That Isherwood was himself aware of and apparently uncomfortable with this tendency in his writing becomes clear if one compares with the opening section of the novel the earlier and separately published

version that appeared in 1959.[4] The former, from which a good
deal of ponderous analysis has been excised, is considerably live-
lier in pace and, furthermore, more in line with the understanding
of Isherwood's protagonist rather than that of his narrator. There
is, however, an inevitability about the relatively less ambiguous
strategies of Isherwood's later novels, given the larger certainties
of his fundamental beliefs; and it is undoubtedly the attempt,
based precisely on these beliefs, to keep simultaneously before the
reader the differing perceptions of his narrator and his protagonist
that accounts for the structural device, in *Down There on a Visit*
as in the novels that immediately precede and follow it, of a
"frame," temporal or stylistic, used to enclose, to distance, and to
comment upon the continuing action of the three novels.

Still, if the double vision of these later novels is more immediately manifest, this is not to say that Isherwood's irony lacks either
subtlety or point, although it is probably true that, as compared
with *The Berlin Stories, Down There on a Visit* replaces density
with range, displaying Christopher's life on a broader but less
concentrated canvas and making possible a diversity of fictional
approaches within the controlling organization of the novel as a
whole. "Mr. Lancaster," the first of the stories, which deals with
Christopher at his youngest and most callow, is, not inappropri-
ately, the simplest and most conventional in design. Built on the
apparent contrast between the twenty-three-year-old protagonist
and his distant and older cousin Alexander, "Mr. Lancaster" re-
verts to a character type and to themes most fully exploited in
Isherwood's first two novels. Like the self-conscious heroes or
antiheroes of those books, Christopher defines himself by anger,
by opposition, and particularly by his hostility to the older generation. Like Philip and Eric, Christopher, whose eagerness for life is
overshadowed by his naïveté and fear, guards himself, as the story's main pattern of images suggests, by "play-acting" (14), his
esthetically neutralizing response to the complexities of his own
subjectivity and the responsibilities of personal relations. Again
and again the keynote is sounded: "To reassure himself," the narrator explains, "he converts [experience] into epic myth as fast as
it happens" (14), and later on he adds: "My entrance upon Act
One of the drama was lacking in style" (16).

The major clue to Christopher's personality appears, however,
not in the recurrent allusions to epic myth and epic drama but in
the more discreetly symbolic reference (embodied in the name of
the ship on which he makes his trip to visit Mr. Lancaster) to
Coriolanus. That Isherwood had in mind those lines in *The Waste*

Land, in which the second voice of the thunder offers its com-
mandment to sympathize,[5] is clear in terms both of the general
significance of the story and of the more specific echo—in Christopher's comment about his cousin: "I just did not have the key to
him it seemed" (55)—of the central phrase in Eliot's passage. "Mr.
Lancaster" is, in fact, predominantly concerned with Christopher's failure of sympathy, the result less of his ignorance and age
than of his egoism, his entrapment, to borrow another of Eliot's
images, within the prison of himself.

Isherwood's success in his story derives in large part from his
skill in deploying the disparate voices and understandings of his
central figure so as to delay and complicate the reader's responses
both to him and to his cousin. It is easy enough at first to accept
Christopher's estimate of Mr. Lancaster as offensive and self-satis-
fied and to bristle empathetically at the older man's attempts to
dramatize himself and patronize his visitor. Only gradually is one
made to feel the pathos of Mr. Lancaster's situation and to recognize the cruelty of Christopher's essential indifference to it. Isherwood's purpose, however, is not primarily to show that his young
traveler is no better as a human being, but that he is no different.
As in *Mr. Norris,* the central irony lies in the resemblances between the two men; and the point, hinted at throughout the story,
is made overtly in the narrator's reflections on its climax, the suicide of Mr. Lancaster: "I think I see now that Mr. Lancaster's
invitation to me was his last attempt to re-establish relations with
the outside world. But of course it was already much too late.
. . . He had lived too long inside his sounding box, listening to his
own reverberations, his epic song of himself" (57). Directly and
symbolically, these lines, even as they summarize the tragedy of
Mr. Lancaster's egoism, underscore, particularly through the
phrase "epic song," the fact that his traits are no more than inten-
sifications or exaggerations of Christopher's. More complex and at
this point more resilient, the younger man moves on, but the
"negative despair" (237), as it is later called, that kills Mr. Lancaster remains as at least one of his possibilities as well.

II   "Ambrose"

The sense of an older and more knowledgeable narrator is least
apparent in "Ambrose," the second and most accomplished of the
stories, about half of which is written in the form of a diary.
Isherwood's aim is not only to make vivid the confusions and
complexities of his protagonist's thought but also to define more
symbolically the relations between time and the self. The empha-

sis on presentness—Ambrose begins: " ... this is May 1933—and here I am, starting on another journey" (61)—corresponds to Christopher's inability to surmount the limits of his ego, to escape temporally, as he tries to do spatially, from the uncomfortable existential reality of his situation.

The need to escape leads Christopher to St. Gregory, where, looking, as he puts it, for "some basis of genuine feeling" (70), he finds, initially at least, still another image of his own negative impulses, which he is too weak to resist but also, in the long run, too weak to sustain. As the symbolic concretion of all the story's meanings, St. Gregory presents to Christopher a temptation—less simple and therefore more seductive than that offered by his cousin—not only to avoid a genuine confrontation with himself and the world but also to accept Ambrose's fantastic heterocosm as a more genuine reality than the world it parodies and inverts. For the island, as Christopher sees it, is no less than an independent and autonomous realm, a kingdom with Ambrose as its exiled Shakespearean king. It is equally true, however, and equally relevant to an understanding of Christopher, that the order of St. Gregory is, in fact, disorder; its ruler, an anarchic lord of misrule, is surrounded by boys who are "inhumanly destructive" and who "delight in any kind of confusion or untidiness" (106).

Ambrose is, in short, both one of "The Lost," as sterile as the people an earlier Christopher meets and identifies with in Berlin, and "absolutely self-sufficient within his own world" (72). He embodies, therefore, an apparent solution to the ambivalent impulses of his visitor, with whom he shares background, age, and, presumably, sexual tastes.[6] And Christopher does indeed move, during his stay on the island, toward something approximating Ambrose's way of life; which is to say that he so successfully puts behind him even his theoretical values as to lose for the time his sense of guilt, and so thoroughly gives in to the unconscious forces within him as to evade his normally oppressive self. But the process is finally incomplete. What Ambrose, "that butterfly with wings of steel" (95), offers to the wavering, vacillating Christopher is, in however bizarre a form, a pattern of absolute commitment to a way of life and its consequences; and it is the intransigent acceptance of his own situation—his aloneness and his being, as he puts it, "dead" (75)—that leads Isherwood to surround Ambrose with a suggestion of saintliness. What Christopher *achieves* is not the coherence of Ambrose's negative discipline but, as some of the final entries in his diary reveal, a state of almost parataxic dissolution, in which the flow of time is evaded only by immersion in a kind of eternal and static now and the burden of identity by a fragmentation of the ego into hundreds of disconnected mirrors of chaotic reality.

Ambrose, then, serves as a criticism as well as a reflection of his guest; but he is ultimately too static a figure to do more than prefigure the transformation of an earthly into a heavenly kingdom. Situated somewhere between Mr. Lancaster's negative despair and the "dynamic despair," later attributed to Paul, " . . . that makes dangerous criminals, and, very occasionally, saints" (237), Ambrose has his place in Isherwood's typology and provides Christopher with as much religious significance as he can now comprehend—or, most likely, *more*, since Christopher is hardly ready at this point even to entertain, however uncomfortable he is with his life, the notion of transcending it. The fact is that Christopher's withdrawal from St. Gregory is not simply a matter of how he responds to the psychological and symbolic attitudes represented by Ambrose. Others on the island, notably Waldemar, his friend of earlier times, and Maria Constantinescu, the interloper into its homosexual world, help to define and even to condition Christopher's decision. Waldemar, whose freedom from human worry, anxiety, and guilt makes him another of Isherwood's animals (reminiscent of Otto in *Goodbye to Berlin*) serves in the story as the major contrast to Ambrose. But whereas Ambrose supplies Christopher with a reflection of what, in part at least, he is, Waldemar remains, as Christopher himself recognizes, an unrealizable because an unreal ideal, an image of what he cannot but would like to be.

However, Christopher at this stage in his life is, in fact, seeking the impossible. Polarized though Ambrose and Waldemar are in the story's symbolic structure, they have in common an essential innocence that moves Christopher to alternate emulation and envy in his attempt to recapture, like Stephen Monk, the un-self-consciousness of a precognitive world. It is Maria who, in pointing out to the not altogether willing or comprehending Christopher his identification with herself, sets the seal of experience on him; and, in so doing, she precipitates, probably more than any of the others, his decision to depart. "We monsters," she tells him cheerfully, "we feel only curiosity. . . . You cannot hold a monster by his emotion, only by puzzling him" (125). All the more ironic in that it recalls Christopher's lack of curiosity toward Mr. Lancaster, Maria's comment isolates the trait, hinted at by the novel's title and later defined by Paul as "tourism," that henceforth provides continuity among the protagonist's various selves and allies him with his counterparts of the 1930's.

Christopher moves on finally, then, because he has completed his tour (in which his role is obviously that of Virgil to the reader's Dante) of the second of the circles of hell that the novel describes. But if he is still the outsider, still the traveler unable to find his home or himself, he is a more knowledgeable one, and the story ends not with the retrospective understanding of the narrator but with the protagonist's own epiphany. Looking into a mirror after his return to England, he notes a new look in his eyes and admits to himself: "I didn't belong on his island"; and then he adds, still more significantly: "But now I knew that I didn't belong here, either. Or anywhere" (135). Anticipatory as well as summary, the comment testifies not only to the growth in Christopher's self-awareness but to the direction, both out of time and away from the self, in which he is hereafter to move; with what degree of success it is not yet indicated.

III   "Waldemar"

Not too much needs to be said about "Waldemar," which in many ways provides, both technically and thematically, an interlude of sorts between "Ambrose" and "Paul." Radically different in its setting, "Waldemar," filled as it is with anticipations of war, is completely the opposite of "Ambrose" in atmosphere as well. Furthermore, as the least symbolic in texture of the novel's episodes, "Waldemar" gains its effect not from the interplay of a series of complex and frequently ambiguous images but from the depiction, first, of the actual fact of the English establishment and, second, of those minor emotions—peevishness, nervousness, sulking—which Isherwood's protagonists so frequently experience and which provide so much of the authenticity of his books.

On the other hand, Christopher's attitudes are not unlike those he expresses at the beginning of "Ambrose," as he leaves Berlin. Just back from another trip, weary, bored, "spinning" (140), he differs largely in the extent of his exasperation with the "old gang." But even as he fulminates against England—an island, it is suggested, no less insular than St. Gregory—he begins to perceive, paradoxically, in his ability to play "The Others' game" (141), the bankruptcy, as a rationale for his own life, of his anger and his need to prove himself to his enemies. The future, predicted for the reader at least by Christopher's loss of political faith and by the violent atheism about which Hugh Weston makes his amused comment: "Careful! Careful! If you keep going on like that, my dear, you'll have *such* a conversion one of these days!" (142), is, however, more than Christopher, hagridden by time and place, can see. What he undergoes and what the story describes is a state of paralyzing crisis, from which the everpresent Waldemar helps, quite unintentionally, to free him.

Most obviously, Waldemar, whose encounters with English officialdom and provincial mores provide the story line of the episode, enables Christopher both to explore and to justify his own feelings about his country. Specifically, as the victim of the composite "image of *authority*" (173) that haunts Christopher, Waldemar brings to its climax his friend's anger against his ancestors and his resolve to reject, with a more conscious finality than when he settles down with Ambrose, their domination over him. Waldemar is, however, not only victim but victimizer, as Christopher acknowledges in his description of him as coarsened and "for the first time in his life, capable of hurting another person" (147).

That Isherwood means in part to trace an inevitable decline in the type represented by Waldemar seems clear: an "angel," as he first appears in "Mr. Lancaster," an animal in "Ambrose," he is in his own story all too human—heartless, cruel, exploitative in his relation with his fiancée, and vulgar in his attempt to assume a more fashionable identity. But something else is at issue: linked more closely than any other character with the world in which he lives, Waldemar, the only character except Christopher who appears in each of the novel's stories, functions not simply as an illustration of what happens to the aging amoralist but as an embodiment of the *Zeitgeist*, unconsciously adapting himself, as neither Ambrose nor Paul can, to the external and mutable conditions whose expression he then becomes.

In this sense, Waldemar is, if more subtly, a symbol of what Christopher means to deny as well as the object of his sympathy; for, as a manifestation of the time spirit, Waldemar suggests as much the England that expels him as the Germany to which he returns, an attitude, that is to say, not restricted to one country but spread through the world at large—the world of egoism expressing itself equally in the impending war and in Christopher's feverish concern with it, in Waldemar's desertion of his fiancée and in Christopher's animal-like sex. And it is that complex of attitudes, finally, that Christopher rejects, although his understanding of the implications of what he does is still minimal. Christopher's decision to leave England is, by intention at least, primarily an act of negation, not of recovery, an attempt to provide his life with still another setting but not yet with a new foundation. It is in "Paul" that Isherwood finally gives his protagonist a glimpse into the world of spirit.

IV "Paul"

But, after all, it is only a glimpse. At the beginning of "Paul," it is true, Christopher has begun to organize his life in a different way: abstaining from cigarettes, alcohol, and sex, he is, as he says, "Now, at last ... playing *my* game, not the game of the Others" (202). And perhaps he is, but the continued use of the game metaphor to express his situation, particularly since he is now a Vedantist, suggests that he is recognizably the same Christopher—the novel's center but not, certainly, its hero. That role belongs rather to Paul, who is intended to be the moral center and "touchstone"[7] of the book as a whole and who, more than any other character in the novel, acts as Christopher's double and the final comment on his limitations.

The complicated relationship between the two men—compounded of hostility and friendship, based on a shifting system of dependencies, mixing a Mortmere-like playfulness with a barely contained sexuality—suggests an attempt, at least in its earlier and closer stages, of each to find himself through the other. But it is clear from the beginning, even at that point where Paul's situation is ostensibly the more critical, that Christopher's need to justify his own existence through vicarious identification with his new friend is by far the stronger. The principle of their likeness once established, it is easy to see that Paul is for Christopher that part of himself which even now doubts or at least resists the claims of Vedanta and to recognize that Christopher associates the likelihood of his own spiritual success with the possibility of change in Paul.

But the main point of the story lies elsewhere: that, for all his enthusiasm, something in Christopher wants, as he later realizes, not to succeed but to fail; that, at whatever level of consciousness, he in fact helps to subvert Paul's progress, thereby freeing himself from at least a strict adherence to the rules he has been following, reveals not only his own ambivalence but also and more importantly the essential, ironic dissimilarity between the two men, which becomes increasingly apparent after the bizarre episode at the retreat but which is implicit from the beginning of the story.

As compared with Christopher—who, for all his inner turmoil, moves easily through a variety of social situations, adjusting himself, on the surface at least, with an ease not far short of Waldemar's to the mores of the various hells through which he passes—Paul, alternately wild, mannered, angry, and jealous, suggests even at his most contained a quality of tension and a depth of response that make him as consistent as and even more uncompromising than Ambrose, with whom he shares the tendency to fear love and provoke aggression. Comfortable only at the edges of the world Christopher generally inhabits, Paul is by turns "the most expensive male prostitute in the world" (194) and a determined ascetic. Far more extreme in either case than Christopher is or can be, Paul in his subsequent response to Christopher's modified practice of Vedanta—"Either be a proper monk, or a dirty old man" (301)—provides a gloss on his own values, particularly on the completeness of his involvement.

Christopher's early observation about Paul—"He didn't belong among the animals" (207)—and Augustus Parr's pronouncement that "We can rise to anything because we can sink to anything" (230) suggest in the by now familiar rhetoric of the novel that the extremes between which Paul operates are those of saint and sinner.[8] Leaving too little, perhaps, to the reader's imagination, Isherwood has his narrator work out the opposition through an accumulation of symbolic images and incidents by comparison with which the texture of "Ambrose" appears a model of chasteness and restraint. Religious overtones, in fact, accompany Paul throughout the story; and although Parr, with his penchant for baroque elaboration, is the source for most of these,[9] still his feeling about Paul is shared by a number of the characters.

It is specifically in this context that there come Paul's reproach to Christopher: "You know, you really *are* a tourist, to your bones. I bet you're always sending post cards with 'Down here on a visit' on them" (315–16)[10] and, more dramatically, the news of Paul's death. In an ending that recalls, formally, the irony of Isherwood's prewar novels, the description of the death is left, after Christopher's laconic announcement of it, to a letter in which one of Paul's friends manages totally to misunderstand and misrepresent him. Nonetheless, Isherwood contrives to leave the reader in no doubt that Paul has achieved, presumably in Vedantic terms, the knowledge and the reality of life after death, the reward, it is implied, that awaits the true experiencer at the end of Blake's "road of excess."

But if Paul's apotheosis supplies an appropriate and even inevitable conclusion to the symbolic structure of *Down There on a Visit*, it also raises a number of significant problems about the book. The question of the nature and viability of the novel's morality is by far the most difficult to deal with, both because of the general critical assumption about the neutrality in literature of subject matter, or even of values as such, and because of the increasing acceptance, especially among intellectuals, of the particular ethical system that *Down There on a Visit* demonstrates. This system, accredited by over a century and a half of writers including Baudelaire, Dostoevski, Huysmans,[11] and Genet, finds its most cogent expression in Eliot's famous formulation: "So far as we are human, what we do must be either evil or good; so far as we do evil or good, we are human; and it is better, in a paradoxical way, to do evil than to do nothing: at least, we exist."[12]

This is not the place to argue the abstract relations of literature and life, but it needs to be recognized what is implied in the case of *Down There on a Visit* by the substitution for a more traditional conception of good and evil of an ethic in which virtue is a function of activity and activity is valued, without reference to intention or result, to the degree that it is extreme. As the novel's kinetic hero and its model of energy and thoroughgoingness, Paul is meant presumably to recommend a way of living as well as of dying, but without his halo of images, he suggests not only something less than a saint but also something more ordinary than a holy sinner. If he is not quite, as one reviewer calls him, "a monster of heartless vulgar egotism,"[13] still there is sufficient truth in the description to make one take a second look at Paul and to recognize that, as a result of his self-concern, he is totally incapable of engaging in or of sustaining any personal relation with another human being. Isherwood refers to Paul's "characteristic sadism" (*Exhumations,* 176), and Christopher to the fact that "he could only do things ... *against* someone else" (303); and it is strikingly true that, however great Paul's need to experience all things to their limit, he shows in human terms only a capacity for great hatred. It is, then, the paradox of the story that, whereas Paul's particular kind of commitment to life is presented to the reader as good in and of itself, it is in fact only the assurance of his salvation that validates his otherwise sterile life.

Some years before the publication of *Down There on a Visit,* and perhaps with that book in mind, Isherwood commented: "If I ever write a religious novel, I shall begin by trying to prove that my saint-to-be really *is* Mr. Jones" (*Exhumations,* 117); and it is clear that one of the major efforts of the story is to persuade the reader that Paul is, if in a somewhat grim and modern sense, both average and ordinary. Certainly, as compared with characters like Huxley's Sebastian Barnack or Waugh's Sebastian Flyte,[14] Paul manages to suggest with his humor and his dynamism that he does in fact embody the qualities the others only symbolize. The problem is rather whether Isherwood succeeds too well, whether in his presentation of Paul's aggressions, his defensiveness, his "sour-ness" (194), and his habitual "camping,"[15] he convinces the reader so thoroughly of Paul's "humanness" as to make it difficult for him to credit his saintliness. As in *The World in the Evening*, though less damagingly, the result of Isherwood's attempt to make the realistic and symbolic aspects of his hero coalesce is an obviously compensatory insistence on the latter, which in "Paul" manifests itself in the imagery throughout and at the close in the melo-dramatic death, the precipitousness of which suggests an attempt to storm the reader's skepticism and win his sympathetic assent to Paul's translation into a better as well as another world.

As the example of Paul indicates, the difficulty that, in varying degrees, the reader experiences in Isherwood's first three postwar novels is not, as in some of the earlier books, a matter of under-standing what is intended but of assenting to what is offered. The problem in *Down There on a Visit* is compounded by the fact that Paul perhaps comes too late on the scene to provide, as he is clearly meant to do, the major focus for the novel as a whole. On the other hand, it is Paul's relative unimportance in the novel and the new prominence of Christopher, as compared with that ac-corded to his predecessors of the 1930's and 1940's, that allows *Down There on a Visit* to survive with only minor scars the literary shortcomings of its hero as *The World in the Evening*, by contrast, so conspicuously fails to survive Stephen Monk's.

Like Waldemar, who, now as a *bon bourgeois*, makes his last appearance in the story, Paul derives his importance finally from the light he sheds on the novel's protagonist; and, as Waldemar confirms through his total ordinariness Christopher's obstinate humanity, so Paul, the extraordinary man, transcending at the last both space and time, authenticates—or at least is meant to—the basis of what Christopher believes. Incapable, as compared with Paul, of knowing "this thing" directly or even of believing in it without reservation, Christopher matures in the course of the novel but, like the protagonists of Isherwood's prewar novels, only to a limited degree. Moving dialectically through the various hells where he meets Mr. Lancaster, Ambrose, Waldemar, and Paul, Christopher arrives, one might say, at a higher level of the spiral his life describes and becomes a better and steadier, certainly a more self-aware individual. But he is not, one is bound to add, a radically different one, and it is ironically fitting that he achieves his final growth vicariously and symbolically through the most flamboyant of his *Doppelgängers*, by whose presumptive triumph he is also judged. But judged or not, it is Christopher who, fictionally at least, wins out, who provides the novel with its esthetically cohesive center and, Paul notwithstanding, with its most convincing moral force. What one regrets as the novel ends is not the death of Paul but the fact that, after five books and a group of ancillary stories, one has seen—to give Christopher the most famous of his names—the last of the much-traveled Herr Issyvoo.

CHAPTER 11

Memento Mori

"**I** FEEL that if I were really George, I would kill myself," Isherwood remarked about the protagonist of *A Single Man* (1964). "Poor devil, what has he got. Nothing!"[1] The judgment may be too harsh in the light of the book itself, but it at least suggests the difference that is intended to exist between the consciousness of George and that of the narrator, who, as most of his predecessors do not, directly establishes the perspective of the novel and makes clear its values. At the same time, it is impossible not to recognize how large the areas of agreement are between George and the anonymous narrator—so much so that for most of the book the latter acts, in Isherwood's phrase, as "a kind of familiar,"[2] shutting down his own awareness and presenting George to the reader as he sees himself. The coincidence of the two minds is in fact a natural one; since strictly in human terms George and the narrator are very much at one, sharing, if not the identical temperament, at any rate a similar one, as well as a variety of attitudes on such matters as middle-class life, American materialism, and sex.

The disparity between the two is of a different order; and as the likeness facilitates the reader's sympathetic identification with George, so the difference makes possible, indeed necessary, a simultaneously more objective and critical view, the immediate cause of which is the narrator's infrequent withdrawal from his complicity with George. The foundation for the novel's double vision is to be found, of course, in Isherwood's religious beliefs, and it is easy to credit Isherwood's admission that George is himself as he might have been, had he not discovered Vedanta.[3] The beliefs in question are overtly formulated only very near the end of the novel when, George asleep, the narrator develops an elaborate analogy of his own, in which the characters are compared to so many rock pools, each apparently "an entity; though, of course, it is not" (183). The pools are seen, in "the night-time of the flood," to lose their distinctness in the indiscriminateness of the ocean, as "in sleep come the waters of that other ocean—that

127

consciousness which is no one in particular but which contains everyone and everything, past, present, and future" (184). The sense of the metaphor is both clear and familiar: even more than the novels that precede it, *A Single Man* insists upon the illusion of separateness and the factitiousness of identity. "The waters of the ocean," the same section ends, "are not really other than the waters of the pool" (184).[4]

What is more interesting to observe is that the problem of explicitness, so often considered in earlier chapters, seems curiously beside the point here, not because of Isherwood's presentation of these ideas—the narrator's exposition is, if anything, more extended and unequivocal than usual—but because of the context that the book as a whole provides for them. Structurally the simplest and most severe of the postwar fictions—limited as it is almost exclusively to the chronological events of one day—and tonally the most somber, despite frequent eruptions of humor, *A Single Man* is also the austerest in its controlling vision. With its uncompromisingly eschatological overview of its protagonist's life, in which death is the most insistent of the last things, the book may be thought of as the least novelistic of Isherwood's novels—indeed, as something more in the nature of a fictionalized sermon. Inevitably, then, the book demands and, to the degree that it is successful, elicits from the reader a different set of expectations and of responses from those he brings to other novels. In this sense, the events of *A Single Man*, however interesting in and of themselves, are to be seen, figuratively if not quite allegorically, as supplying an *exemplum*, in which George's day becomes a metaphor for his life, and George himself a type of everyman. And in this sense too, the narrator's parabolic disquisition on the rock pools and the ocean comes not, as it would in *The World in the Evening*, as the gratingly didactic underlining of a point already made dramatically but as the anticipated fulfillment, so to speak, of the congregation's expectations.

The argument can no doubt be pushed too far: the largest part of the novel is, after all, devoted not to the great ocean but to the individual rock pool and the relation of the rock pools to one another. And, in his concern with the problems of human identity and personal relations, Isherwood provides, against the background of a world as thick and multitudinous in texture as an Antonioni film, a variety of moods and scenes that effectively establishes, quite apart from their symbolic and ironic meanings, the alternating rhythms of an apparently random, normal day. Nonetheless, although the spiritual dimension of the novel is made completely manifest only in its final pages, Isherwood clearly means for the reader to be aware of it throughout, and nowhere more than in the opening of the novel where, as in the exordium of a sermon, both subject and perspective are established.

I   The Nature of Identity

Half-philosophically, half-physiologically, *A Single Man* begins with a meditation on identity, defined in its first lines as the product of existence in time: "Waking up begins with saying *am* and *now*" (9). The word *now* is central, here and in the novel as a whole, and, as always in Isherwood's books, thoughts of time lead to an awareness of death and an accompanying reaction of fear. What is new in *A Single Man* are the intensity of both and Isherwood's insistence, registered through a number of different techniques, on the mortality of his character. Clinical and impersonal, the narrator traces the emergence of "this live dying creature" (10–11) from the undifferentiated state of sleep through the beginnings of his daily ritual, from situation in time to location in space, until, with the final awareness of others or of himself as others see him, he resumes his accustomed place in the upper limits of the normal ego world, where the assumption of a public personality seems to promise a respite from the terrors that precede the full birth into consciousness.

Conditioned by point of view and tone, the reader observes the spectacle of George, naked and afraid, with detachment; and the reaction that these techniques together establish, style further enforces. Internal stylistic variation, specifically as it relates to diction, is indeed the clue to much that happens in the novel, since style mirrors the major changes in George or in the ways we are invited to perceive him. Referred to variously throughout the opening section as "that," "the body," "the creature," and "it" (9–11), George suggests a specimen of sorts, the appropriate object of disinterested and scientific curiosity to some more than human presence. On the other hand, it may be misleading to maintain that the examination is altogether dispassionate: if much of the vocabulary—"cortex," "pylorus," "vagus nerve," and so on —has in and of itself the neutrality of technical jargon, it still suggests in context—the context of George urinating, "nauseated by the pylorus in a state of spasm" (10)—not only an interest in but something of a disgust for the human body, reminiscent in a general way of the later novels of Aldous Huxley, in whom also an otherworldly vision entails a scatological treatment of this world. The comparison, however, although invited by Isherwood's use of

Huxley's *After Many a Summer Dies the Swan* in his own work, is valid only to a limited degree. Sharing Huxley's ironic and metaphysical view of existence, Isherwood displays in his novel none of the former's excessive revulsion from humanity, or the gratuitous loathing for the body that increasingly mars Huxley's religious fiction; and ultimately the strength of *A Single Man* is that, although the "now" of George's barely conscious state echoes throughout, it functions not as a simple condemnation of life but, more equivocally and complexly, as a *memento mori,* an intermittent reminder both for the reader and for George.

With the transformation of its protagonist from "it" to "he," the second stage of the novel gradually begins. Coordinated with a general change in technique—most apparent in the relaxation and humanizing of the tone; in the normalization of the diction; and, above all, in the increasing identification of the narrator with the novel's central figure—George's progress, first in thought and then in fact, into the world of other people describes a movement, never quite complete, from human animal to social being. Looked at in this way, George bears a marked family resemblance to Isherwood's other protagonists: vain, human, lonely, doing what he does because he "can imagine no alternative" (10). But the sense of separateness, as the novel's title indicates, bears down more heavily upon him: isolated not only by the mere fact of being human—by sharing, that is to say, what Isherwood sees as the common lot of men, each trapped in his individual ego—George, an English expatriate, an intellectual, and a homosexual, is in addition an outsider in "the American utopia, the kingdom of the good life upon earth" (26).

George is "single" also in a much starker and more immediate sense. The first steps of his ascent into daily consciousness are marked by a descent into memory, a brief and painful awareness, physical even before it is mental, of the recent death of his lover: "he stops short and knows, with a sick newness, almost as though it were for the first time: Jim is dead. Is dead" (13). But it is not his loss that sets George apart from the characters in all of Isherwood's other novels; it is rather the fact of his life with Jim, for alone among these, it is only he who knows, or has known, fully and completely, the experience of loving another human being.

That the first relationship in his books to deserve that name takes place, as it were, off stage, may be attributed to Isherwood's literary and perhaps psychological tentativeness in dealing with, for him, a new kind of interpersonal situation or, equally and more demonstrably, to the dramatic requirements of the novel. What is significant, however, is the effect on the book of Jim's virtual absence from it and of George's continuing love for him. And Isherwood's skill in portraying the latter is such that *A Single Man* conveys a breadth of sympathy and a depth of feeling altogether new to his fiction.

Roughly speaking, George's attitude to his environment is determined, to use Vedantic terms, by his aversions and his addictions: by what he lacks or hates and, more obliquely, by what he loves or wants. The simplest and most painful fact of George's experience, of which Jim, or the memory of him, is of course the proximate cause, is loneliness. *A Single Man* is filled with symbols of his feeling, from "Charlotte's nest" (120) on Soledad Way to the supermarket where, briefly and deceptively, "brightness offers sanctuary from loneliness and the dark" (112). George's own house is like an island, not facing the road and separated from it by a bridge, a visible proof to him, now that he is alone, that he is also "a prisoner for life" (15). But the acuteness of George's suffering is the measure of his reaction, and the fantastic orgies of hatred in which he indulges as he drives along the freeway represent, in however negative a fashion, his determination to maintain his hold on life: "Rage, resentment, spleen," George thinks (or perhaps the narrator does), "—of such is the vitality of middle age" (40).

What is most interesting to observe about George's anger is that its objects are in some fundamental sense a reflection of him; the Christmas decorations, the suburban mores, the deodorants, and the other paraphernalia of the American way of life express not only the crassness of a material civilization but also the effort, which is his as well, to ignore time and death. For George is, as the classroom discussion of *After Many a Summer* makes clear, Tithonus, a less crude and perhaps a less honest version of Huxley's Jo Stoyte or the fifth Earl of Gonister: "A withered boy" (106) furiously intent on putting off age by devoting himself to the pursuit of *now*. His ambition mirrored in the use throughout the novel of the present tense, George, like some Vanitas figure in a medieval painting, is at his happiest during the day in the "easygoing physical democracy" (109) of the gym, where with satisfaction he recognizes, after a detailed survey of his body, that "*he hasn't given up*" (106).

Never more complacent or self-deceived than he is here in Isherwood's comic representation of the earthly paradise, George is, however, something more also. Flanked on either side by scenes of death and change, the episode in the gym is pivotal in

forming and complicating the reader's reactions to him. Driven to
go there, "although this isn't one of his regular days" (104), by
recoil from his visit to a dying friend in the hospital, George,
resolutely exercising, takes on an admirable, almost a heroic quality. And, as his frantic contention with time gives way to an anti-
climactic drive through the Los Angeles hills, where, as in the
other sections of the book, his own decay is represented by the
surrounding urban landscape, the pathos as well as the irony of
George's proud assertion that he is among "the ranks of that mar-
velous minority, The Living" (103) becomes all too apparent.

George is minority conscious throughout *A Single Man*, but not
in any simple or even consistent way. Most obviously, his identification with society's other outsiders relates itself to his fury
against the philistine majority, and particularly, if not exclusively,
to its attitudes toward homosexuals.[5] Subtle and honest enough, at
times, to recognize that, as victim, he is himself implicated in the
destructive process, he lectures to his class on the psychology of
aggression: "While you're being persecuted," he tells them, "you
hate what's happening to you, you hate the people who are making it happen; you're in a world of hate" (72). But George's discussion of minorities, however admirable and sophisticated its
liberalism, constitutes still another assertion of the claims of his
own individuality. It is Isherwood who, by way of pointing out
another impulse in his protagonist of which George is, at least
consciously, unaware, makes the seemingly paradoxical connection between tolerance as a human value, with its suggestion of
respect for diversity and even separateness, and the religious vision of humanity unified beyond the barriers of the self. The belief is left implicit in *A Single Man*, but a conversation in *After
Many a Summer* makes clear the nature of the relationship:

"But, heck," said Pete, "you're always talking about democracy. Doesn't
that mean respecting personality?"
"Of course, " Mr. Propter agreed. "Respecting it in order that it may be
able to transcend itself. Slavery and fanaticism intensify the obsession with
time and evil and the self. . . . The more you respect a personality, the better
its chance of discovering that all personality is a prison."[6]

George is, and remains, incapable of recognizing his prison, but a
good deal of the novel is devoted to suggesting his unacknowl-
edged desire to escape from it. Thus minorities are made to symbolize the need of the ego not only to maintain but also to
overcome its illusory singleness: to be, impossibly, one and other.

The claims of the self to be whole and undivided are disposed of easily and comically. No more an entity than he is eternal, George proliferates in the course of the novel into a host of subsidiary characters—the chauffeur figure, the talking head, the actor-teacher, and others—all of them trying at various times to elude "old guardian Cortex" (146).

And the process of dissolution is made manifest in other ways as well: hinted at throughout, it becomes clearest at that point when George, having only half-humorously characterized Americans, himself included, as "essentially ... creatures of spirit" (92), undergoes a change that ironically belies his description: "All of a sudden, he is much, much older. ... He hums queerly to himself, with a sound like bees around a hive. From time to time, as he walks, he emits quite loud, prolonged farts" (93). Subject, then, to the division of body and spirit and to the whims of his alter egos, whose increasing autonomy marks the decline in his own powers of control, George, like the swarming waters of the rock pool, is diversity masquerading as unity, though with a growing lack of success as his day draws to its end.

II   The Loss of the Self

This subversion from within of the ego's unsteady rule finds its more positive counterpart in George's relationships with others. The clue to these is provided once again by George's life with Jim and particularly by his memory of his lover "lying opposite him at the other end of the couch, also reading; the two of them absorbed in their books yet so completely aware of each other's presence" (115). The state of equilibrium that both the physical disposition and the mental attitudes of the two men describe is unique in *A Single Man*, but the tensions that are resolved by it are not. With Jim's death, the need for separateness apparently dissociates itself from and predominates over the need for connection, and George's subsequent relations tend to reflect a lack either of closeness or of understanding. It is increasingly apparent, however, that separateness is as delusive as singleness and that, whatever George understands by his effort to maintain his individuality, Isherwood means to suggest that George's general withdrawal from intimacy of any kind paradoxically broadens even as it depersonalizes his sense of fellowship with the larger human community—and ultimately with what the reader at least recognizes, against the background of the novel's religious beliefs, as the oceanic consciousness later described by the narrator.

This is not to suggest a total reorientation of George's personality after Jim is killed. His recollection of "that glorious Indian summer of lust" that he and Jim spent, with many others, on the beach, "each group or pair to itself and bothering no one, yet all a part of the life of the tribal encampment" (148), articulates an earlier stage of George's desire to be apart from, even as he is part of, the world of people around him. But George's detachment from the group is at this point predicated on the existence and presence of Jim and on the harmony of their love. Jim gone, George's relationships move perceptibly toward the impersonal. So, as he walks by two of his students, he "feels that his day has been brightened" (76–77) by their waving: "The old steamship and the young castaways have exchanged signals—but not signals for help. They respect each other's privacy. They have no desire for involvement" (76). Later at the gym, he is hailed in passing by some casual acquaintances, "and this George feels, is the most genuinely friendly greeting he has received all day" (106). Even his sexuality —imaged first in the tennis match that "stirs George into hot excitement" (53) and whose rules make possible the symbolic overthrow of the majority (the big blond boy) by the minority (the smaller Mexican boy) and then in the masturbatory fantasy, George's last conscious act, in which, with the same two boys now in his mind's eye, "he begins passing in and out of their writhing, panting bodies. He is either. He is both at once" (179–80)—even this, though necessarily more direct, is no more personal.

This is perhaps to simplify things to a degree. Watching the tennis match, George is moved by the desire to see the blond boy "vault over the net, and force the cruel little gold cat to submit to his marble strength" (53), to transform the game, that is to say, into a more intimate confrontation. And one of George's last thoughts is that "he will find another Jim ... he will because he must" (182). But without denying to George the reality of his wants and his hopes and without attributing to him the knowledge that belongs to Isherwood and the narrator, one can still recognize how consistently his aim is to achieve not a positive relationship but a state of being: a stasis of emotion in which the particularity of himself or of others is accepted—as the Mexican's is by the rules of the game—and even transcended.

The point can be made best with reference to George's two most extended and symbolic contacts, those with his friend Charlotte and his student Kenny. George's feeling for "Charley" is based partly on a sense of their common plight—like him, she is lonely; "like him, she is a survivor" (120)—and partly on his response to what she represents: England, the past, *his* past, with

"the heartbreakingly insecure snugness of those nursery pleasures!" (14). But if Charley, in her sentimental evocation of earlier
days and her talk of returning home to her roots, crystallizes one
of George's choices, her real importance in the novel and in George's life lies elsewhere: in creating for him, precisely because she
does *not* understand him, the state of what he calls *la felicidad,* a
happiness totally his own, "this utterly mysterious unsensational
thing—not bliss, not ecstasy, not joy" (123), which is capable of
coexisting not only with Charley's obtuseness but with her personal misery.

George's more complex relations with Kenny constitute both a
summary and the climax of his day. Coincident with an impulse
that takes George, "with the movement of a child wriggling free
of a grownup" (146) toward the ocean and with another change
in technique, brought about this time by an increasing density of
images, by a generally more concatenated style, and finally by the
narrator's assumption of an enthusiastically lyrical tone, Kenny's
appearance at The Starboard Side precipitates, with the help of a
good deal of liquor, the release of George's daytime restraints.
Intended, too obviously perhaps, as Charley's opposite, Kenny
represents youth, the future, and inevitably, if only for a moment,
death. But his more important function obviously is to generate, as
Charlotte does the "woman-created" (123) *felicidad,* the mascu-
line state of "dialogue," in which "what really matters is not what
you talk about, but the being together in this particular relationship" (154). The relationship is further defined, in a way that
shows it to be the closest approximation to the type of freedom
George seeks from others, as the encounter of "symbolic figures.
. . . Because the dialogue is by its nature impersonal" (154). George's achievement, the attainment of a state so abstract that by
comparison not only his love for Jim but even the opposition of
the two tennis players seems heavy with human feeling, proves
nevertheless to be illusory. Whether the instability is that of the
dialogue itself—and George is afraid that Kenny does not in fact
understand the nature of their meeting[7]—or whether it reflects his
own ambivalence, the relationship, almost immediately upon its
realization, clearly begins to undergo a series of changes.

The rapid succession of these changes and their variousness
suggest that they, not George's ambiguous relationship with
Kenny, are the main issue. Describing no pattern of logical development, they serve rather to actualize what is already potential in
George: to bring to the surface, in all its contradictory and mutually exclusive force, the whole content of his inner life. Indeed,

the ideas of transformation and paradox dominate this entire section of the novel, all of which takes place, appropriately, in the vicinity of the protean and all-embracing ocean; and in its central episode, where Isherwood's style is at its richest and most poetic, George encounters "the stunning baptism of the surf" (162).

The symbolic implications of George's immersion are far from simple: both by convention and because of the narrator's later elaboration of the water image, the reader is directed most obviously toward "that other ocean" in which the ceremony of rebirth finds its eternal fulfillment. And yet, although George in undergoing these "rites of purification" (162), "washes away thought, speech, mood, desire, whole selves, entire lifetimes" (162–63), one has not been led to contemplate his final release from the Great Wheel or even to see him, given his overwhelming concern with the here and now, as in a state of spiritual preparedness. That, in a more neutral sense, the scene looks forward to George's death is clear; but the end of his day is still somewhere in the future. And in the light of what follows the episode on the beach, it appears that George's baptism is intended to signal also a change in human terms that provides, if not a solution to his problems, at least a liberation of all that is best in him.[8]

The apparent inconsistency between the mundane and the transcendental associations of George's trip "across the border into the water-world" (163) is resolved in the last, "person-to-person" phase of his relationship with Kenny, where the increasing stress on the disparity between the physical and the spiritual that runs through the remaining pages of the novel is complicated by the use of the former, conceived of specifically in sexual terms, as a metaphor for the latter. So, in what is manifestly intended as his major speech, George says to Kenny: "It's the enormous tragedy of everything nowadays: flirtation. Flirtation instead of fucking, if you'll pardon my coarseness. All you ever do is flirt. ... And miss the one thing that might really ... *transform your entire life*—" (176–77). As an apostle of wholeheartedness, George is reminiscent of Paul; but George, less angular and uncompromising, more fallible and human, is a more attractive figure. If his defense of experience is made credible by contrast with Kenny's fundamental detachment, as well as by the quality of his own life, it is made vivid and funny by the contrast between his overly rhetorical lecturer's manner and the drunkenness that is its inspiration. Furthermore, the masturbation that follows, in final contrast to Kenny, or rather to his coy, teasing letter, and as a practical demonstration of George's speech, has its comic side too in George's frantic attempt to find suitable actors for his fantasy: Kenny "isn't taking his lust seriously; in fact, he seems to be on the verge of giggles" (179).

Nevertheless, although George's words and deeds are humorously qualified at the last by the narrator and by George as well, one accepts his evaluation of himself, delivered smilingly but "with entire self-satisfaction": "Yes, I *am* crazy. ... That is my secret; my strength" (180). Intensity is always a positive quality in Isherwood's world; and if George differs from Paul, he differs as well from the Christophers who precede him in his determination to face life head-on. Putting behind him in his last barely conscious moments— "Partial surfacings" (181) is the narrator's phrase, in anticipation of George's imminent reunion with "the darkness of the full flood" (184)—Charley, Kenny, and even Jim, the past, the future, and death, George sounds for the final time his keynote: "It is Now that he must find another Jim. Now that he must love. Now that he must live... "(182). And if one not only accepts but takes seriously George's strivings, it is because Isherwood too takes seriously, on its own level, the world of Forsterian liberalism in which his protagonist lives. That as a writer becomes more religious he may also become more humanistic and more humane is the lesson of Isherwood's career; and George, the most sympathetic of his protagonists, is also the most successful product of his double vision.

But double it remains; and in the final pages of the novel George's proud determination, and with it the whole world of liberal humanism, are judged from the perspective of death and eternity—and found wanting. With a return to the technical strategies of the opening scene, but a reversal of its content, Isherwood has his narrator describe the process whereby George's identity is unmade, his life ironically destroyed in the moment, as it seems to George, of its fullest possession.[9] The account of George's death is indeed a multiplication of ironies. The reintroduction of an even more severely medical vocabulary; the etiology of George's heart failure, in which the beginnings of the disease are assigned to the instant he first sees Jim, so that ugliness and death are not, as George thinks, hidden in the future but implicit in the past; the use of the word *Now*, heretofore the condition of his identity and the object of his most intense search, as a prelude to George's attack—all lead to the final, ironic dichotomy that is implicit throughout the novel, between the body as so much perishable stuff, "cousin to the garbage in the container on the back porch," and the spirit, "away out there on the deep waters" (186), as everlasting.

Too distant and dispassionate to be cruel, Isherwood's irony conveys, however, an enormous sadness.[10] But even this is neutralized by his brilliant device of making the death hypothetical, by only supposing "that this is the night, and the hour, and the appointed minute" (186). Melodramatic in *Down There on a Visit*, death in *A Single Man* is symbolic, in that the supposititiousness of the event only underlines its inevitability and also the irrelevance of its precise time from the perspective that the narrator now adopts. Further, the significance of George himself is generalized by his problematic death: no longer a single man, he is, more than at any other point in the novel, everyman, a mirror of the common fate.

As the novel ends, then, its subject becomes in a sense not George at all but the reader; and indeed none of Isherwood's other novels points the reader so resolutely back to himself. *A Single Man* offers at its close no comfortable certainties—none, at any rate, on this side of the grave—no opportunities to speculate on the protagonist's future, to patronize or moralize over him. There is no occasion, in short, for the reader to imagine that he is himself other than "this live dying creature." And if Isherwood's novel is a sermon, it may be thought to end with Baudelaire's words: "—Hypocrite lecteur,—mon semblable,—mon frère!"

CHAPTER 12

The Play of Maya

MOST CRITICISM, concerned as it is with order and coherence, with pattern and symmetry, is inescapably teleological. Thus the obvious temptation to regard an author's final writings as the inevitable goal of his career or, if he is still productive, to treat his latest work as if it were his last. Still, the temptation, whatever it may owe to a desire for shapeliness, is hardly to be resisted in the case of *A Meeting by the River* (1967), which suggests, through the history of one of its characters, a summary of Isherwood's intellectual and emotional development and which, even more obviously, is pervasively reminiscent of his earlier work. It is nothing new, of course, to find Isherwood mining his previous fiction:[1] in however slight and unobtrusive a way, there is throughout Isherwood's career a suggestion, half-playful, half-ironic, of writing for a group of initiates able to respond, when coming upon familiar bits of his fictional landscape, with the amusement and pleasure of recognition.

But the process is more extensive in *A Meeting by the River*, to which almost all of the preceding novels are made to contribute a character, an incident, a situation, or at the least an already inhabited house.[2] More to the point, because probably less intentionally, the two brothers who are Isherwood's chief concern in the book recall insistently and variously, but without losing their own integrity as characters, most of the protagonists of the earlier novels and, still more, Michael and James Ransom of *The Ascent of F 6*. For *A Meeting by the River*, whatever else it is, is the fullest expression of Isherwood's abiding interest in The Truly Weak Man, or rather in the variations on that type, which leads him here once again to explore the phenomenon of doubles.

As usual, the most reliable guide to Isherwood's thematic concerns is found in his handling of technique, all the more so in this book since in none of the others is form so completely congruent with vision. In fact, for all its resemblances to the earlier fiction and drama, *A Meeting by the River* represents technically a new departure for Isherwood. At the moment, what is at issue is the treatment of the novel's narrative element: the presentation exclusively through the agency of diary entries and letters of what is probably Isherwood's most minimal plot. *A Meeting by the River* is not, strictly speaking, a symbolic novel or even in any important way a novel with symbols; nevertheless, the shape of the book can be said in itself to represent—with the strict economy of means that is in evidence throughout and that makes one wish to place it in the tradition of the French rather than of the English novel —Isherwood's conception of his leading figures. So, while the diary suggests the inevitable medium for a scrupulous and self-conscious solitary like Oliver, who is bent on an intransigent examination of conscience, to carry on a dialogue with himself,[3] Patrick's letters illustrate both his need to enter into relationships with others and the extraordinary flexibility that leads him so easily to adapt his reports, frequently of the same incident, to the tastes and expectations of his three correspondents.

The differences between the brothers supply the principal, if not finally the most profound, concern of the novel. These are illustrated formally by the various ways in which the two express themselves and by the quality of the prose that they typically employ (Oliver's being the more supple and controlled, Patrick's the more descriptive and rhetorical); and the differences are further heightened by a series of more casually elaborated contrasts —ironist and sentimentalist, saint and sinner, moralist and immoralist—made throughout the novel. The opposition is, however, less simple than it seems at first sight. The obviously defensive irony that characterizes Oliver—"our greatest living master of understatement" (112) is his brother's description of him—points, for example, even more than it does in Isherwood's novels of the 1930's, to an urgent desire to move beyond the constrictions of the self. And the flagrant sentimentality upon which Patrick so self-flatteringly congratulates himself clearly expresses as much the need to conceal as to expose himself. In short, the reader is made gradually to distrust the categories offered to him and to question, with an increasing sense of the complexity of the task imposed on him, the self-awareness, the percipience, and ultimately the relative worth of the two brothers.

The problems of interpretation that arise in connection with an unreliable narrator—that already familiar figure of Isherwood's first-person novels—are of course doubled in *A Meeting by the River,* if indeed the term "narrator" can be used at all for characters who are not in any ordinary sense telling a story. In any case, it is to Oliver, whose sincerity at least is never in doubt, that one is inclined to look first for some sort of guidance. But there is a good deal more at stake than simple fidelity to fact as Oliver sees it. However beside the point it may be in assessing the truth of Oliver's vocation, however crassly reductive it may be in its approach, Patrick's rational and psychological analysis of his brother as both inordinately ambitious and deeply guilty about his ambition rings true as a reading of unconscious motivation.[4] And Isherwood is nothing if not anxious in this novel to give the devil, as whose agent Patrick sometimes playfully sees himself, his due. Furthermore, there is the question of human appeal as opposed to what may be thought of as abstract virtue; and it is in this area that Isherwood most thoroughly complicates the reader's responses to his protagonists. Oliver, for all his honesty, is something of a prig, not only touching but also occasionally boring in his sensitivity and vulnerability; and there is something less than attractive in his easily aroused jealousy and hostilities and in the tight and rigid approach to life that he describes as the "desperate conscience-stricken urge to *keep busy*" (117).

If Oliver is compulsive and puritanical, essentially unchanged in personality even after he becomes a monk, Patrick is his opposite, dissolute and conscienceless, if not as passionate or uncontrolled as he likes to imagine in his self-dramatizing way. But although he is far more vain, far more conscious of his age and body than even George in *A Single Man,* although he is irritating in his archness and frequently repellent in his treatment of others, where self-deception seems at times to turn into gross and ruthless hypocrisy, still the reader is invited to respond, as Oliver is on occasion able to do, to "the get-away-with-murder impudence with which he accepts the best as his absolute right" (115). Clearly Patrick is another of Isherwood's animals: unworriedly inconsistent, worldly, above all facile; a far more mercurial and therefore more interesting character than his brother; an egoist whose Norris-like charm and gusto almost neutralize the outrageousness of his behavior. It is difficult to know, as one observes him in his letters equivocating and smoothly rearranging the facts of his experience to suit his own convenience, whether one is to laugh uproariously or to pass moral judgment; it is only clear that, if one condemns the man, one can hardly fail to applaud his art.

In any case, the complexities of Oliver's and Patrick's characters and the unlikeness of the two are sufficient to account for the persistent failures of communication that are the basis for much of the novel's irony, arising as it does from the disparate accounts the brothers give of one another and of the experiences they share or

have shared. Furthermore, what is revealed of their attitude to
their mother, herself another carryover from the earlier work, suggests the source of their mutual mistrust, rivalry, and antagonism.
The sense of division manifests itself throughout the book but, as
one might expect, nowhere more than in relation to Oliver's decision to take his final vows. The insecurities that, at different levels
of consciousness, afflict both men, lead to Oliver's need for Patrick's approval and, as Oliver analyzes it, somewhat more complexly to Patrick's need for his brother's failure. Each, that is to
say, seeks from the other, tacitly or explicitly, the assurance, that
his way of life is the correct one; or to put it another way, each
attempts, by way of insuring the integrity of his own beliefs, to
subvert those of his brother.

It is not Isherwood's intention, however, simply to contrast
monk and libertine or to polarize abstractions of the order of right
and wrong or good and evil. Obviously, the threat each feels reflects, at some basic level, an attraction to what the other represents, a response, in other words, to what is even more
fundamentally internal than external. So Oliver at least, as always
the more astute and self-aware, is ready to acknowledge, with an
ironic consciousness of how it reflects on the goal of his Vedantic
studies, his sense of the bond between his brother and himself: "I
get afraid," he confides to his diary, "that I'll start behaving like
him and lose my own identity altogether—which is pretty funny
when you think that my whole life in the Monastery is aimed
toward mortifying the sense of ego!" (115).

More than this, Isherwood's aim is to show that the two men in
fact parallel or complement each other. Oliver's comment—
"Heredity has made us part of a single circuit, our wires are all
connected" (115)—supplies an apposite metaphor for the intrica-
cies of the relationship, but it is the concept of The Truly Weak
Man that comes closest to making intelligible its exact nature. It
will be remembered that in *Lions and Shadows* Isherwood describes the protagonists of his projected novel, *The North-West
Passage,* as "two halves or aspects of the same person ... but,
while Tommy will one day be lost in trying to force the North-
West Passage, Roger will never even dare to attempt it" (211).
Isherwood's reworking of the same theme some thirty years later
necessarily reflects his postwar beliefs—Oliver, to be sure, dies,
but only in a spiritual sense, presumably to be reborn; and Patrick,
although he shares his prototype's reluctance to broach the unknown, is at least in danger of salvation by the end of the novel
—but both versions agree on the fundamental identity of the two

men who fulfill their destinies in such apparently opposed ways.

In *A Meeting by the River* the connection between the brothers becomes clearest when one compares the "visions" that each has in the course of the novel. In some sense, the whole of Oliver's life in the monastery may be thought of as a progress toward the realization of his desire to put behind him his ordinary self by achieving the Vedantic vision so often described in the last several chapters, and Patrick uses the word in just this way when referring to his brother's beliefs (12). But more dramatic is the latter's experience, "intensely vivid, far more so than an ordinary dream" (172), in which, after suffering a near-collapse as a result of Patrick's analysis of his motives, he sees his Swami and feels "happy and at peace" (173). The knowledge that comes to Oliver is, as one would expect, of unity: "I knew that Swami was 'dead', and I knew that nevertheless he was now with me—*and that he is with me always, wherever I am* . . . now we are never separated" (173).

The relationship is meant of course to symbolize and prefigure the oneness of all being in the enlightened state, but Patrick's corresponding experience, couched though it is in appropriately and violently sexual terms, is neither in its quality nor in its substance markedly different: "This was much more than a dream," he writes to his lover Tommy, who is its object, "it was so intense it was a sort of vision" (130); and he then explains that "this life I got a glimpse of was of such a closeness as I'd never even imagined could exist between the two human beings, because it was a life *entirely without fear*" (131).

Both brothers, then, express the desire of their deepest selves to overcome isolation. What is more interesting is that each is somehow involved in the other's thoughts. Oliver's "communication" leads to an awareness of his Swami's concern for Patrick and to the belief, as he puts it, that "the three of us belonged together intimately" (174). Patrick, characteristically more self-seeking, informs Tommy: "I'm certain that *you* could be my brother—the kind of brother I now know I've been searching for all these years" (131–32). That Patrick abruptly terminates his relationship with Tommy after the latter's importunate telephone call suggests an element of inconstancy in him that one gathers has heretofore characterized Oliver, intellectually rather than sexually, as well, but it does not belie the content of his dream; rather it indicates that his homosexual affair satisfies only one of his needs, a need that once again Oliver shares with him. So, in a subsequent letter to his obviously long-suffering wife, Patrick writes: "To me you are safety and freedom" (185); and in his last diary entry, Oliver, who has already found safety in his decision to become a monk, echoes his brother in his comment on the ceremony of taking final vows: "it's entering into freedom" (188).

What remains to be determined, given the similarities and the dissimilarities of the brothers, is the degree to which each affects the other, the degree to which they are changed by their confrontation and particularly by the meeting, to which the title of the novel refers, in which Patrick confesses to his affair and unsettles Oliver's hold on his beliefs. At the least it seems possible to say that the brothers accept each other more fully: Oliver's inclusion of Patrick in the mystical communion of himself and his Swami is matched by Patrick's own sense, as he writes to his wife about his brother, of "such closeness in the thought of us three together" (182) and by his secretly keeping his own vigil during the night of Oliver's vows. Further, there is a moment of genuine resolution in Patrick's unexpected gesture of reverence to his brother after the ceremony and in the embrace that follows—a blending, as it were, of East and West and of the comic and serious: "His lips just touched my ear in a sort of kiss and he whispered, 'Well Olly, you've *really* gone and torn it now!' And I whispered back, 'Looks like I'm stuck with it, doesn't it?' " (190).

Nonetheless, it is clear that, however moving this rapprochement, each of the brothers is fated to pursue the path he has marked out for himself. And inevitably so: Patrick, in a more than usually honest mood, expresses his fear that "life will begin to appear in its usual complex muddle as soon as I return to a more normal environment" (178); and Isherwood, writing more abstractly in *An Approach to Vedanta*, explains pertinently that "each psychological type—and, indeed, each separate individual —has the peculiar ethics and responsibilities which are dictated by its nature. ... A man must go forward from where he stands. He cannot jump to the Absolute; he must evolve toward it" (57– 58). Exactly what Patrick's place is in the process of evolution must remain a matter of speculation, but Oliver at any rate comes to feel, thanks to his vision, that "Patrick had got himself into a spiritual state which was very serious, so serious as to be almost ridiculous, but that nevertheless *he would be all right*" (175). The final irony of the relationship is that each of the brothers at the last sees the other in his own terms:[5] Oliver comes to feel that his brother is "in a state of grace" (177); Patrick, that Oliver "will gradually evolve into one of those terrifyingly uncorrupt politico-religious leaders who appear from time to time to be adored by

millions, dominate international conferences and finally check-
mate the opposition by getting themselves assassinated!" (181).

This process of mutual self-projection—along with the disconcerting fact that Patrick, only a matter of hours before Oliver has
his vision, tells his brother that he "might even have been forced
to invent" (153) the Swami, if he had not met him—helps to focus
the troublesome question of how one is to determine the accuracy
of either brother's statements and assumptions. Is one, for example, to regard Oliver's sight of his mentor as a self-induced, because needed, delusion, his vocation as his ambiguous response to
his ambition; and can Patrick be regarded, however tentatively
and unconsciously, as expressing in his devious maneuvers a dissatisfaction with his own life? The answer appears to be that one
cannot in fact tell, that there are no clues to guide the reader; and
it becomes increasingly evident that, in such matters at least, truth
is not only undiscoverable but irrelevant as well: the answers,
curious as the assertion appears at first sight, do not make any
difference.

These remarks seem to suggest that Isherwood's own vision is
relativistic, and, in a limited sense, this is true. The total absence
of a mediating narrator in *A Meeting by the River* implies a different conception on Isherwood's part of his role in relation to his
characters and necessarily makes different kinds of demands on
the reader, who is both involved, as the novel's characters are, in
the exploration of human or psychological truth and at one with
the hidden author in his transcendence of, one might almost say
his indifference to, that truth. Any reader of Isherwood's earlier
novels is, of course, used to adopting a perspective based on double vision; but for all its subtlety, the irony of the 1930's works is
of a different kind: more limited and self-enclosed, more personal
in its relation to Isherwood himself. The achievement of *A Meeting by the River* is Isherwood's ability to accept, with a tolerance
very different from that displayed by the protagonists of the prewar, first-person novels, the varieties of human behavior and the
many paths that lead to the knowledge of ultimate reality. In fact,
the objectivity, the cameralike view of the human scene that William and Christopher claim, falsely, in *The Berlin Stories,* is realized only in his most recent book, where, even more than in the
other Vedantic novels, characters are seen with an equal if not
quite disinterested eye.

This is not to say that Isherwood ceases in *A Meeting by the
River* to be very much a moralist, but the ethical judgments of the
book exist to a large degree independently of considerations

found not only in the early novels but even in those that immediately precede it. Certainly Oliver is meant to be seen as closer to a realization of what Isherwood takes to be man's goal in life; but it does not follow, as it does in Paul's case, that he is therefore the hero of the novel or the more creditable of the two brothers. Isherwood's point seems to be that all men, however unwillingly in some instances, are striving, along their own lines, for a knowledge of their true selves and, the novel perhaps implies, must come to it in the end.

In aid of this belief, Isherwood introduces Vedanta into *A Meeting by the River* not only as the basis of its value system but, more than in any of the other postwar novels, as part of its human content. Rhetorically, Isherwood's strategy is obvious enough: presented with the contrast between Oliver and Patrick on the one hand and on the other the relaxed, humorous, and unaffected monks, whose presence unobtrusively pervades the novel, the reader is invited to accept the latters' simplicity as a pledge of their integrity and also of that of the system to which they adhere. Since it alone, in the crosscurrents of the novel's accounts of life at the monastery, is never called into doubt, an affirmation is clearly intended; and that affirmation is meant to resolve and put into perspective the complexities of the brothers' lives. Both bear witness, Patrick more grudgingly, to the effect of the monks on them, and both betray the self-consciousness that marks their distance, even Oliver's, from them. But it is the direction of their lives, finally, that is significant—and thus the centrality of Oliver's recognition: "What separates me from them isn't important, not ultimately. What unites is the one and only thing that really matters" (120).

Whether Isherwood succeeds in making the reader accept his monks as persuasive characters and therefore as adequate vehicles of his belief is another matter. The objection of one reviewer is largely true, that "at the heart of the book there is a blur: the underlying religious assumptions are insufficiently dramatized ... and have to be taken too much on trust."[6] Nonetheless, Isherwood's partial failure in coordinating the metaphysical and the human dimensions of his novel is not sufficient to detract from its essential success or to obscure its underlying belief, which, put forth in *An Approach to Vedanta*, is that "each of us has, so to speak, one foot in the absolute and one in the relative" (68). The assurance of the existence of the Atman, the underlying reality, is common to all of Isherwood's postwar novels, is indeed what lends to the five otherwise diverse books a recognizable unity. But only gradually, and with an increasing amount of success from the time of *Down There on a Visit* onward, does Isherwood come to terms with the world of human activity, seen in its relation to the Absolute as "the Divine play of Maya" (137).

Perfected at last in *A Meeting by the River,* the feeling that the phenomenal universe has "only a relative existence" (*Vedanta,* 68)[7] accounts both for Isherwood's tone in that novel and for his forbearance, one might call it, toward his characters. It is, for example, as an inhabitant of the world of Maya and against the transcendental background of Vedanta that Patrick can be said to exist in a state of grace; and in this sense too he emerges as equal in importance and worth to his brother. "At that moment," Oliver writes after he takes his final vows and as he embraces Patrick, "I seemed to stand outside myself and see the two of us, and Swami, and the onlookers, all involved in this tremendous joke" (190). And Oliver's attitude, no less serious for its cosmic laughter, is surely Isherwood's as well.

CHAPTER *13*

Critical Perspectives

I
N A mood of amusement, or perhaps of bravado, Isherwood's
English publishers featured in their advertisement of *Down
There on a Visit* a series of ten critical comments on the novel, half
of them favorable, half adverse. The balanced, antithetical remarks about the book neatly summarize the difficulties that critics
have experienced in "placing" Isherwood in the ranks of modern
writers. The problem is, in fact, a double one: if some critics have
failed to detect the pervasive moral intention that gives to his
writings their continuity, others have failed to detect the equally
significant differences between the prewar and the postwar
books. Not surprisingly, whatever agreement can be found in assessments of Isherwood's works centers on the novels of the
1930's, and particularly on *The Berlin Stories*, since these are, and
were even at the time, taken to represent the very spirit of the
decade. Undoubtedly, Isherwood (along with Auden and Upward)
helped to give definitive shape to the characteristic mythology of
the 1930's and managed, in his explorations of prewar Germany,
successfully to transform private fantasy (the Mortmere world of
Lions and Shadows) into a public examination of what the writers
of the 1930's recognized as the illness of their times.

But to praise Isherwood for his ability to subsume the private
sensibility of the 1920's to the journalistic immediacy required by
a more agitated and hectic decade is to give too much value to the
reporter at the expense of the novelist. Isherwood's lucid, understated style, his gift for spare and rapid narrative, his eye for the
first, premonitory symptoms of disease in England and on the
Continent, are all, in the final analysis, pressed into the service of
an overarching irony, directed not so much at the world as at the
self in its relation to that world. Chronicler of his decade's destructive impulses, Isherwood is still more (and like Auden) the
diagnostician of the ego at war with itself. Eschewing the political
certainties of Upward and Day Lewis, he remains, for all his ties
with the "committed generation," its most subtle explorer of the
inner life.

In fact, Isherwood is concerned throughout his career with the ego's attempts to overcome its detachment and to break through to the genuine forms of life. But not always in the same way. The undoubted originality of Herr Issyvoo and, more generally, of Isherwood's re-creation of prewar Germany has been allowed for too long to haunt and confuse critical assessments of Isherwood's subsequent works and to blur the honesty and ingenuity of what, seen in retrospect, has been not only a long-range but also a *developing* literary experiment in detecting the disguises and subterfuges of the protean self. What needs to be stressed is that, after *Prater Violet*, Isherwood moves more and more toward an exploration and testing of extremes. Thus the special autobiographical mode that he first adopts in *Mr. Norris* for trapping the shifting linguistic strategies of the ego is thematically broadened in the postwar fiction by his choice of a new metaphysical perspective and is rendered more complex by means of the narrative and stylistic techniques he devises to articulate his double vision.

What is finally at issue, however, is not the superiority of Isherwood's postwar to his prewar fiction but the recognition of where and how, in both parts of his career, he succeeds. Not that success is uniform in either group of novels: the occasional lack of density in texture and feeling that characterizes some of the earlier books is balanced by the slackness and pale self-imitativeness of *Prater Violet;* the ambiguities which sometimes mar the novels of the 1920's and 1930's, by the conceptual inadequacies of *The World in the Evening.* But the immediacy of response that marks the author of *The Berlin Stories* as the most percipient observer of his generation is to be found as well in Isherwood's explorations—the most acute, surely, of the postwar period—into the psychology of religious belief. And if he is not alone in bringing to the literature of the 1930's a new awareness of social and political concerns, nor, more recently, in enlarging the willingness of fiction to deal with sexual and metaphysical themes, still, comparison with analogous figures (Orwell or the members of the Auden group in the earlier period; writers as diverse as Huxley, Truman Capote, and Gore Vidal, in the later) makes clear how substantial Isherwood's originality is nonetheless.

But Isherwood's most remarkable achievement has to do with the inventiveness and versatility of his handling of technique, which are apparent in his command of stylistic, and particularly syntactic, subtleties; in his structural and verbal ironies; in his experiments with narrators of varying degrees of insensitivity or reliability; in his narrative use of letters and diaries; and, finally, in his shifting temporal perspectives. Indeed, Isherwood's success in finding new forms (or revitalizing old ones) makes of him one of the most rewarding and subtle experimental novelists of the last four decades.

Isherwood's range is, however, ultimately less important than the fact that all of his techniques are carefully used to force the reader into discovering and constructing for himself the shape of character and meaning. It is a risky enterprise for a novelist to make demands of this kind, not only because he is likely to find the sluggish reader entangled by his own preconceptions and insensibilities, but because the author may, as Isherwood sometimes does, scatter too few clues to point even the perceptive reader's way. The risk is one that Isherwood shares with ironic novelists in general, from Jane Austen to E. M. Forster, and particularly with Forster, from whose work his own, in this sense, as in so many others, most clearly derives.

But comparison with Forster, however inevitable, can be misleading. Certainly, Isherwood begins his career, as he has acknowledged, as Forster's imitator (in *All the Conspirators*). During the 1930's Isherwood may more accurately be described as Forster's heir: paring down, as he does, Forster's "vernacular" style; rendering both more critical and equivocal his irony; developing still further the problem of the self in a state of crisis. But Forster's persistent values of moderation, balance, and proportion are increasingly alien to the concerns of Isherwood's fiction, just as his narrative methods are increasingly irrelevant to an understanding of Isherwood's technique; and, if Forster's influence continues even into Isherwood's later novels, it is an attenuated one, apparent largely in matters of style and tone.

Indeed, even in the earlier period, where not only Forster's but also Lawrence's and Joyce's influence can be found on the conception or composition of a number of Isherwood's works, the usefulness of comparison with other English novelists is limited. Finally, it is the tradition of the French *récit* that most adequately suggests, particularly in matters of literary form, the shape of Isherwood's novels. From Benjamin Constant to Gide and Camus, the short, spare, concentrated *récit* provides a genre in which personal and metaphysical problems fuse. Expressing, in its structure and its narrative strategies as in its themes, the moral dilemmas, hesitancies, and ambiguities of a society in which absolute values have begun to give way, it asks that the reader sustain a close critical awareness not only of what is being stated, and how, but, equally, of what has been omitted. Isherwood's demands are the same, and where he is most assured—as in *The Berlin Stories* and in the two latest of his novels—it is in this highly intellectual and elegant form that he excels: still today, as in the 1930's, the understated and discreetly probing conscience of an age of verbal inflation.

It is impossible to guess exactly what Isherwood's work will be like in the future. Although *A Meeting by the River* can be seen as putting the seal on the change that becomes apparent in his writings after his emigration to the United States, it marks only the latest stage in the development of his attitudes and responses, from the anger of his earliest novel to the capacious and comprehensive sympathy of the latest. Isherwood has said, however, that his next book will be an autobiography; and it is likely that *A Meeting by the River,* in recording the events of Oliver's life, predicts the main lines of that story. For Oliver, one gathers from such works as *Lions and Shadows, An Approach to Vedanta,* and *World Within World,* resembles, far more than those of his predecessors who share their author's name, Isherwood himself. And, as one pieces together the events that lead Oliver, not without hesitations and uncertainties, toward his journey's end in India, one becomes aware of watching as well Isherwood's own progress, from the concern with the "old gang" that dominates the earlier works to the knowledge, which transforms both his later writings and his life, of the God within. It is the ego that provides Isherwood with his first and most abiding theme; appropriately enough for one of the century's most brilliantly ironic moralists, it is in its loss that his work is renewed.

Notes and References

Chapter One

1. All references to Isherwood's novels and plays, as well as to *Exhumations, An Approach to Vedanta* (referred to as *Vedanta*), and Auden's *Collected Poetry* will be given in parentheses immediately following the material quoted. Full bibliographical information on these works can be found in the next section.

2. See Wayne C. Booth, *The Rhetoric of Fiction* (Chicago, 1961), pp. 67–77.

3. See Chapters IX and X of *Enemies of Promise and Other Essays* (Garden City, New York, 1960). The first two quotations at the end of the paragraph appear on p. 76 of this edition, the third and fourth on pp. 83 and 82, respectively.

4. Roughly speaking, the difference between Romantic and modern irony lies in the fact that, whereas the former celebrates the freedom of standing above, the latter records the inability to enter in. In both there is detachment and overview, but the Romantic rejoices and the modern despairs. To the one, detachment is power; to the other, it is impotence and failure: freedom becomes alienation and superiority to the world becomes separation from it.

5. "To Reinhold and Ursula Niebuhr," *Nones* (New York, 1950), p. 7.

6. Chalmers is modeled after the novelist Edward Upward; Hugh Weston corresponds to Auden, Stephen Savage to Spender, Philip Linsley to Hector Wintle. See *Exhumations*, pp. 172–73.

7. "Byron: The Making of a Comic Poet," *The New York Review of Books*, VII (August 18, 1966), p. 14.

8. "A Conversation on Tape," *The London Magazine*, I, New Series (June, 1961), 42.

9. Stephen Spender, *World Within World* (London, 1951), p. 126.

Chapter Two

1. "Introduction," *All the Conspirators* (London, "Traveller's Library," 1939), p. 7.

2. *Great English Short Stories* (New York, "Laurel Editions," 1957), p. 185.

3. In *Lions and Shadows*, Isherwood claims that he chose the title simply because "it sounded grand" (p. 262), and in "A Conversation on Tape," he says: "I just thought it was a beautiful Shakespearian phrase" (p. 50).

4. See Joseph Warren Beach, *Obsessive Images: Symbolism in Poetry of the 1930's and 1940's*, ed. William Van O'Connor (Minneapolis, 1960), particularly pp. 119–31, and Monroe K. Spears, "The Dominant Symbols in Auden's Poetry,"*Sewanee Review*, LIX (1951), 392–405.

5. The poem is "Journey to Iceland" and appears in *Letters from Iceland* by Auden and Louis MacNeice (New York, 1937), p. 26. In *Collected Poetry*, p. 8, "Unreal" has been changed to "A refuge."

6. See in my book, *Art and Order: A Study of E. M. Forster* (New York, 1964), the discussion of what I have called "the aesthetic view of life," p. 11 and Chapter 2, *passim*.

7. The poem is number XXII of *Poems* (London, 1950), p. 74. It originally appeared in the 1933 edition of *Poems*.

8. In *Lions and Shadows* Allen introduces Isherwood to *Les fleurs du mal*. In his own novel, *In the Thirties* (London, 1962), Upward gives another and more disturbed portrait of Chalmers, now called Allen Sebrill. Isherwood himself translated Baudelaire's *Intimate Journals* in 1930.

Isherwood made this comment about Allen in an interview with me on January 13, 1964. Hereafter the conversation will be referred to as "Interview, 1964."

9. The first quotation is from Rex Warner's "Sonnet," *Poems* (New York, 1938), p. 13; the second is from Stephen Spender's "Not palaces, an era's crown," *Collected Poems* (New York, 1955), p. 50; the third is from C. Day Lewis's *The Magnetic Mountain, Collected Poems* (London, 1954), p. 107; and the last is from another poem by Warner, also called "Sonnet," *Poems*, p. 4.

10. "August for the people and their favourite islands," *Look Stranger!* (London, 1946), pp. 65–66. The italics are mine.

11. *New Country* (London, 1933), pp. 19–20.

12. *Journey to the Border* (London, 1938), p. 5.

Chapter Three

1. See the chapter on "Pattern and Rhythm" in Forster's *Aspects of the Novel* (London, 1953).

2. *Tradition and Dream* (London, 1964), pp. 236–37.

3. Frederick R. Karl in *The Contemporary English Novel* (New York, 1962) ascribes Isherwood's particular treatment of time to an imitation of Huxley's *Eyeless in Gaza* (p. 291), although Huxley's novel was published four years later than *The Memorial*. The fact is that Huxley is probably in Isherwood's debt, as Jocelyn Brooke conjectured some time ago in a British Council pamphlet on Huxley (London, 1958), p. 24.

Within the four sections of the novel, Isherwood carries even further the shifts in time by the frequent use of flashbacks. These help to make dramatic the impact of the past on the present, the sense of the present's roots in the past. Isherwood's own explanation of what he meant to achieve by his handling of time appears in *Lions and Shadows*, pp. 397–98.

4. An example is Paul West, who in *The Modern Novel* (London, 1963), p. 78, sees Isherwood and Maugham as authors who "collect the facts, the fascinating copy, and hinge it all carefully into non-committal albums."

5. See *The Rhetoric of Fiction*, pp. 111–12 and *passim*.

6. "Socialism and the Intellectuals," in *The Beat Generation and The*

Angry Young Men, ed. by Gene Feldman and Max Gertenberg (New York, 1959), p. 332.

7. See *Lions and Shadows*, pp. 207–8 and the discussion of The Truly Weak Man in Chapter 1.

8. *Poems*, p. 93.

Chapter Four

1. "The Leaning Tower," *The Moment and Other Essays* (London, 1952), p. 120.

2. *Ibid.*, p. 119.

3. "Books in General," *The New Statesman and Nation*, XLIV (August 23, 1952), 213.

4. *World Within World*, p. 202.

5. The phrase is from the opening line of "In Me Two Worlds." See *Collected Poems of C. Day Lewis*, p. 129.

6. "The Leaning Tower," p. 118.

7. For similar remarks see "A Conversation on Tape," p. 49 and *"Mr. Norris and I* by Gerald Hamilton," *Exhumations*, pp. 86–87. Hamilton is the model for Norris.

8. *The Rhetoric of Fiction*, p. 74.

9. *World Within World*, p. 101.

10. The statement appears in the Penguin edition of *Goodbye to Berlin* (Harmondsworth, Middlesex, 1962), p. 6.

11. "A Conversation on Tape," p. 46.

12. The remark is from a letter quoted in John Lehmann's *The Whispering Gallery* (New York, 1955), p. 225.

13. "The Challenge of Our Time," *Two Cheers for Democracy* (New York, 1951), p. 57.

14. "Interview, 1964." Isherwood went on to say: "One produces vortices."

15. See the exactly contemporary story, "The Turn Round the World" (reprinted in *Exhumations*), which is constructed around the principle of doubles.

16. *Tradition and Dream*, p. 237.

17. Isherwood and others testify to his enthusiasm for Germany and the Germans before and on his arrival in the country. See the unreprinted articles "The Youth Movement in the New Germany," *Action*, I (December 10, 1931), 18; and "German Literature in England," *The New Republic*, LXXXXVIII (April 5, 1939), 254–55. Spender says in *World Within World*, p. 104, that Isherwood "spoke of Germany as the country where all obstructions and complexities of this life were cut through."

Chapter Five

1. *The English Novel: Form and Function* (New York, 1956), p. 131.

2. Norman Friedman in "Point of View in Fiction: The Development of

a Critical Concept," *PMLA*, LXX (December, 1955), 1178–79, sees in the use of "The Camera" as a kind of point of view "the ultimate in authorial exclusion. Here the aim is to transmit, without apparent selection or arrangement, a 'slice of life' as it passes before the recording medium." For Friedman, *Goodbye to Berlin* is an example of the slice-of-life novel, of which he disapproves. In an interview with Harvey Breit, collected in *The Writer Observed* (New York, 1961), Isherwood explicitly attributes the statement to the narrator (p. 141).

3. Penguin edition, p. 6.

4. "A Conversation on Tape," p. 43.

5. "Books in General," p. 213.

6. This is to suggest only that there are biographical resemblances between Peter's life and Spender's. For Isherwood's denial, see "A Conversation on Tape," p. 45.

7. *World Within World*, p. 124.

8. "Books in General," p. 213.

9. Spender's comments on the relationship between Isherwood and Gisa Soloweitschik (the model for Natalia) provide an interesting comparison with the relationship in the book. Spender notes an "Oriental sense of untouchability in Gisa." See *World Within World*, pp. 127–28.

10. *New Writing in England* (New York, 1939), p. 25.

Chapter Six

1. Isherwood's other writings during the 1930's include book reviews, some essays and translations, and a handful of stories. The most important of these are included in *Exhumations*.

2. See B. C. Bloomfield, *W. H. Auden: A Bibliography* (Charlottesville, Virginia, 1964), p. 31; and George Wickes, "An Interview with Christopher Isherwood," [hereafter, "An interview"] Shenandoah, XVI (Spring, 1965), 42.

3. *World Within World*, p. 202. The quotation continues: "We were the Divided Generation of Hamlets who found the world out of joint and failed to set it right."

4. *The Dog Beneath the Skin* was apparently based on an earlier play by Auden called *The Chase*. The poetry is by Auden, who, according to Bloomfield, "identified Act I, scene ii, with the exception of the song, about half of Act II, scene i, and the Destructive Desmond episode as being by Isherwood" (p. 14). How much each of them was responsible for the rest of the play is unclear: Bloomfield quotes Isherwood as affirming, Auden as denying "that most of the play is by Auden" (p. 14).

Bloomfield concludes, on the basis of Isherwood's remarks about the composition of *The Ascent of F 6* that "the prose is Isherwood's and the poetry Auden's" (p. 17), which suggests, as one would suspect in any case, that Isherwood's presence is most to be felt in this play. Of *On the Frontier*, Isherwood has said in "A Conversation on Tape": "I think there's more of Auden's work in *On the Frontier* than any of the plays, because he not only wrote all the poetry but also a big share of the prose" (p. 51).

5. See Bloomfield, p. 17, "An Interview," pp. 40–41, and "A Conversation on Tape," p. 51.

6. *The Making of the Auden Canon* (Minneapolis, 1957), p. 167.

7. "The Auden-Isherwood Collaboration," *The New Republic*, CXLI (November 23, 1959), 16.

8. There is an anticipation of these actions between the first and second scenes of Act III.

9. *New Writing in England*, p. 35.

10. "Interview, 1964."

11. See Julian Symons, *The Thirties: A Dream Revolved* (London, 1960), pp. 82–84.

12. "Letter to Lord Byron," *Letters from Iceland*, p. 58.

13. There is a review of a book of reminiscences about Lawrence in *Exhumations*, pp. 22–24. See also Isherwood's comments on Lawrence in *The Condor and the Cows*, p. 199.

14. "Interview, 1964."

15. "The Auden-Isherwood Collaboration," p. 17.

16. "This ship is like a hospital," the account begins. See *Exhumations*, p. 144.

17. Connolly, *Enemies of Promise*, p. 82.

18. Evelyn Waugh, *Scoop and Put Out More Flags* (New York, "A Laurel Edition," 1961), p. 249. See also, Lehmann, *I Am My Brother*, pp. 30–31.

Chapter Seven

1. Christopher begins as "the good Virgil" (p. 36) to Bergmann's Dante, but later he says of their trips through London: "He was always the guide, and I the tourist" (p. 76).

2. Quoted in Lehmann's *I Am My Brother*, p. 154.

3. "An Interview," pp. 48–49.

4. For Connolly's comments, see Chapter 1.

5. I am referrring specifically here to pp. 177–85. Pages 185–86 provide still another shift in the technique of the novel.

6. *The Book: On the Taboo Against Knowing Who You Are* (New York, 1966), p. 95.

7. Albert Camus, *Le Mythe de Sisyphe: Essai sur L'Absurde* (Paris, 1953), p. 15.

8. See "A Conversation on Tape," p. 52.

Chapter Eight

1. The best accounts appear in *An Approach to Vedanta*, in Isherwood's contribution to the symposium, *What Vedanta Means to Me*, ed. John R. Yale (London, 1961), pp. 38–49; and in his introduction to *Vedanta for the Western World* (New York, Compass Books Edition, 1960), pp. 1–28.

2. *Anatomy of Criticism* (Princeton, 1957), p. 42.

3. As Isherwood has been quick to point out, he produced during these years a large quantity of nonfiction, including *The Condor and the Cows,* a travel book, several translations of Vedantic works, and a number of collections of essays, including some of his own, on Vedanta. See "A Conversation on Tape," p. 52.

4. *World Within World,* p. 301.

5. See below, the discussion of *A Single Man.*

Chapter Nine

1. *The Ample Proposition* (London, 1966), p. 32.

2. The lines are from the first stanza of Donne's *The Progresse of the Soule.*

3. That the context of *The World in the Evening* is specifically Quaker may be explained, even apart from the autobiographical basis of this part of the book, by Isherwood's statement in *An Approach to Vedanta,* p. 46: "The Society of Friends is, as far as I am aware, the Christian Sect which comes closest to agreement with the teachings of Vedanta." Isherwood goes on to say (p. 47): "I suppose that, if I hadn't already met Prabhavananda, I might have become a Quaker."

4. *Fools of Time: Studies in Shakespearean Tragedy* (Toronto, 1967), pp. 3–4.

5. The whole of the sonnet (Number XCIV) is relevant to an understanding of Stephen.

6. "Interview, 1964."

7. "A Conversation on Tape," p. 50.

8. See *An Approach to Vedanta,* pp. 59–62.

9. Cf. Isherwood's comment on Katherine Mansfield, who is a model for Elizabeth Rydal, in *Exhumations,* p. 72: "Mansfield left us also—in her journal, her letters and her recorded biography—the human example of one who dedicated her whole being and existence to the perfection of her work. Only the greatest men and women have the courage to do this; and the degree of their success is of secondary importance."

10. In the preceding paragraph Isherwood writes: "On the chain of attachment the padlock, so to speak, is egotism. . . . Get the padlock open and you have achieved nonattachment. You now know that you are the Atman and that every action is done for the sake of the Atman alone."

11. The famous discussion of "Camp" in the novel (pp. 109–11) takes up the question of the Quakers' lack of style and elegance.

12. "A Conversation on Tape," p. 48.

Chapter Ten

1. In "An Interview" (pp. 46–47), Isherwood said: "No. I doubt very much if I shall use that thing again. This fictional Christopher Isherwood got absolutely too big for his britches and became rather unmanageable, I thought."

2. In this *New Yorker* story, reprinted in *Exhumations,* pp. 230–37, one sees Isherwood suffering most obviously from the "change of accent" to which he admits in "An Interview," p. 35.

3. For an adverse criticism of Isherwood's style in *Down There on a Visit,* see Richard Mayne, "Herr Issyvoo Changes Trains," *New Statesman and Nation,* LXIII (March 9, 1962), 337.

4. *The London Magazine,* VI (October, 1959), 17–54.

5. See lines 411–16 and Eliot's equally apposite reference to F. H. Bradley in his note to the passage. In *Lions and Shadows* (p. 206), Christopher records, in his notes for a projected novel, *The North-West Passage,* the following ideas: "The Epic Myth. . . . People's attitudes to their own Coriolanus-myth."

6. In the light of Ambrose's attempt to set up on his island an ideal homosexual society, there seems to be considerable irony in the choice of names in this section of the book: St. Gregory, of course, reformed monastic discipline and enforced celibacy; St. Ambrose wrote against marriage and displayed a lifelong obsession with asceticism.

7. "Interview, 1964." Isherwood went on to say of Paul that he "brings out the untruth in all of us."

8. Paul's "dynamic despair" is said to be something "which no animal has or can have" (p. 237).

9. See Gerald Heard's curious and relevant book, *The Five Ages of Man* (New York, 1963), in which he discusses, for example, "the high association between genius and epilepsy" (p. 271) and more generally the postindividual or Leptoid man (pp. 81–92 and *passim*). The description is particularly interesting in connection with Paul's impotence and his death. Heard is obviously the model for Augustus Parr.

10. It is at about this point in the novel that there originally appeared the pages which shortly before its publication Isherwood excised and later published in *Exhumations* (pp. 241–54, and see Isherwood's explanatory note, pp. 175–76) as "A Visit to Anselm Oakes." The story describes Christopher's horrifying experience with drugs, the result presumably of his tourist's attitude, and comments on the evil of the uninvolved.

11. The title of Isherwood's novel refers, of course, to Huysmans's *Là-Bas,* which encloses the story of Gilles de Rais, a particularly gruesome type of the sinner-saint, in a plot that describes how through Satanism—or a belief that such a thing exists— two characters come, or almost come, to Catholicism.

12. Eliot's remarks appear in his essay on Baudelaire, which served as the introduction to Isherwood's translation of the *Journaux Intimes.* The quotation can be located most easily in the *Selected Essays* (New York, 1950), p. 380.

13. Julian Jebb, "Down There on a Visit," *London Magazine,* II (April, 1962), 89.

14. The sinner-saints of *Time Must Have a Stop* and *Brideshead Revisited,* respectively.

15. The problem of "camp" is much more insistent with respect to Augus-

tus Parr, a frequently fascinating and amusing figure whose mannerisms sometimes make him hard to take or to take seriously, despite Isherwood's obvious attempt to make the reader believe that although, or because, "he's humanly vain, and he's no fool . . . at the same time he really believes—" (p. 209).

Chapter Eleven

1. "An Interview," p. 52.
2. "Interview, 1964."
3. Isherwood made the comment during a reading of parts of *A Single Man* on January 12, 1964 at the New York YMHA.
4. Cf. *An Approach to Vedanta*, p. 20, where Isherwood uses the same metaphor to express the relation between self and non-self, and Huxley's *Eyeless in Gaza* (New York, 1961), pp. 421–22, where the distinction is made between "the separate waves, the whirlpools, the spray" and "below them the continuous and undifferentiated expanse of the sea."
5. "I have never in my life written specifically about homosexuality," Isherwood said in "An Interview" (p. 52), "—not what I would call writing about homosexuality. What I have done in this particular novel is to write, among many other things, about minorities. And the homosexuals are used as a sort of metaphor for minorities in general."
6. *After Many a Summer Dies the Swan* (New York, n.d.), p. 91.
7. Earlier in the novel George has a brief encounter with Kenny that produces "a kind of intimacy" (p. 82) but no understanding. George's hope at least in the dialogue is for the opposite results.
8. Heard in *The Five Ages of Man* has a good deal to say about the effect of water on man and about its power to bring about "an enlarged state of consciousness" (p. 208).
9. Heard describes "the patient who is at the extremity of individualism" as one who "often dies from heart rupture or brain artery lesion before he knows he is ill" (p. 227).
10. Stanley Kauffmann writes in a review of *A Single Man:* "It is thus a sad story, kept from being a thoroughly moving one because, for one reason, we have a consciousness of its *intent* to be sad." *The New Republic,* CLI (September 5, 1964), 24. The remarks that follow in the text are intended in part as an answer to Kauffmann's objection.

Chapter Twelve

1. One thinks, for example, of the reappearance of Ashmeade in *Prater Violet* or of Mary Scriven in *The World in the Evening*. See "A Conversation on Tape," p. 46.
2. There are, to cite only a few examples, references to Anita Hayden, a minor character in *Prater Violet* and to Chapel Bridge, Eric's family home in *The Memorial* and Christopher's in *Down There on a Visit;* an episode in *All the Conspirators* (pp. 63–64) is called into service, and so is Stephen Monk's work for the Quakers.

3. Oliver's two letters early in the novel—they are his only ones—are required to re-establish his relationship with his brother and to get the plot underway.

4. The allusions to T. E. Lawrence in the novel once again suggest a connection between Oliver and Michael Ransom.

5. Stanley Kauffmann makes this point in his review of the novel, "Passages to India," *The New Republic*, CLVI (April 15, 1967), 37.

6. John Gross, "A Question of Upbringing," *The New York Review of Books*, VIII (May 18, 1967), 36.

7. In the same place Isherwood writes that Maya does "not *mean* illusion, but from the absolute viewpoint . . . [is] illusion."

Selected Bibliography

In cases where the first edition of one of Isherwood's works has not been used, the date of original publication is given in parentheses.

PRIMARY SOURCES

1. *Novels and Autobiography*

All the Conspirators. New York: New Directions, 1958 (1928).
The Berlin Stories. New York: New Directions, 1954 (*The Last of Mr. Norris,* 1935; *Goodbye to Berlin,* 1939).
Down There on a Visit. New York: Simon and Schuster, 1962.
Lions and Shadows: An Education in the Twenties. Norfolk, Conn.: New Directions, 1947 (1938).
A Meeting by the River. New York: Simon and Schuster, 1967.
The Memorial: Portrait of a Family. Norfolk, Conn.: New Directions, 1946 (1932).
Prater Violet. New York: Random House (Modern Library Paperback) n.d. (1945).
A Single Man. New York: Simon and Schuster, 1964.
The World in the Evening. New York: Random House, 1954.

2. *Works Written in Collaboration with W. H. Auden*

Journey to a War. London: Faber & Faber Ltd., 1939.
On the Frontier. New York: Random House, 1938.
Two Great Plays by W. H. Auden and Christopher Isherwood. New York: Random House (Modern Library Paperback), n.d. (*The Dog Beneath the Skin,* 1935; *The Ascent of F 6,* 1936).

3. *Works Relating to Vedanta*

An Approach to Vedanta. Hollywood: Vedanta Press, 1963.
"Discovering Vedanta," *The Twentieth Century,* CLXX (Autumn, 1961), 64–71.
Essentials of Vedanta. Hollywood: Vedanta Press, 1969.
How to Know God: The Yoga Aphorisms of Patanjali. Translated with Swami Prabhavananda. Hollywood: Vedanta Press, 1962.
"Introduction." *What Religion Is in the Words of Swami Vivekananda.* Ed. John Yale. London: Phoenix House Ltd., 1962.
Ramakrishna and His Disciples. New York: Simon and Schuster, 1965.
Shankara's Crest-Jewel of Discrimination. Translated with Swami Prabhavananda. Hollywood: Vedanta Press, 1946.

161

The Song of God: Bhagavad-Gita. Translated with Swami Prabhavananda.
New York: Mentor Books, 1960 (1944).

Vedanta for Modern Man. Ed. Christopher Isherwood. New York: Collier
Books, 1962 (1951).

Vedanta for the Western World. Ed. Christopher Isherwood. New York:
The Viking Press, 1960 (1945).

"What Vedanta Means to Me." *What Vedanta Means to Me.* Ed. John Yale.
London: Rider & Co., 1961. Pp. 38–49.

4. *Miscellaneous and Uncollected Works*

"Aldous Huxley," *Aldous Huxley, 1894–1963.* Ed. Julian Huxley. New
York: Harper & Row, 1966. Pp. 154–62.

The Condor and the Cows: A South American Travel-Diary. New York:
Random House, 1949.

"The Day at La Verne," *The Penguin New Writing,* XIV (July-September,
1942), 12–14.

Exhumations: Stories, Articles, Verses. New York: Simon and Schuster,
1966.

"Foreword," "The Railway Accident," by Allen Chalmers [Edward Up-
ward]. *New Directions in Prose and Poetry,* XI. New York: New Directions, 1949. Pp. 84–85.

"German Literature in England," *The New Republic,* LXXXXVIII (April 5,
1939), 254–55.

Great English Short Stories. Ed. Christopher Isherwood. New York: Dell
Publishing Co. (Laurel Edition), 1957.

"High Valley Theatre," *Theatre Arts,* XXXI (June, 1947), 64–66.

The Intimate Journals of Charles Baudelaire. Trans. Christopher Isherwood. Hollywood: Marcel Rodd, 1947 (1930).

"Just a Gigolo," *The Saturday Review,* XXXV (April 12, 1952), 38. According to Isherwood, "this is actually a translation of the German version
of the song—which I *think* was the original version."

"Notes on a Trip to Mexico," *Harper's Bazaar,* LXXXI (June, 1947), 80–81,
134–36.

"Souvenir des Vacances," *Oxford Poetry.* Ed. W. H. Auden and C. Day
Lewis. Oxford: Basil Blackwell, 1927. P. 48.

Threepenny Novel by Bertolt Brecht. Trans. Desmond I. Vesey. Verses
trans. by Christopher Isherwood. New York: Grove Press, 1956 (*A
Penny for the Poor.* London, 1937).

"The Youth Movement in the New Germany," *Action,* I (December 10,
1931), 18.

SECONDARY SOURCES

ALLEN, WALTER. *Tradition and Dream.* London: Phoenix House, 1964.
Concentrates on the 1930's novels, which are seen as Isherwood's best
work.

AMIS, KINGSLEY. "Socialism and the Intellectuals," *The Beat Generation and The Angry Young Men.* Ed. Gene Feldman and Max Gertenberg. New York: Dell Publishing Co., 1959. A consideration of the political 1930's and the non-political 1950's, with some interesting remarks on the Auden group.

BANTOCK, G. H. "The Novels of Christopher Isherwood," *The Novelist as Thinker.* Ed. B. Rajan. London: Dennis Dobson Ltd., 1947. Sees Isherwood as a comparatively negligible figure with a disproportionately large reputation.

BEACH, JOSEPH WARREN. *The Making of the Auden Canon.* Minneapolis: The University of Minnesota Press, 1959. Chapters 13–15 deal with the Auden-Isherwood plays.

———. *Obsessive Images.* Ed. William Van O'Connor. Minneapolis: The University of Minnesota Press, 1960. Brilliant study of recurrent poetic images in the 1930's.

BLOOMFIELD, B. C. *W. H. Auden: A Bibliography. The Early Years Through 1955.* Charlottesville: The University Press of Virginia, 1964.

BREIT, HARVEY. *The Writer Observed.* New York: Collier Books, 1961. Includes a chatty interview with Isherwood.

CONNOLLY, CYRIL. "Comment," *Horizon,* I (February, 1940), 68–71. An editorial comment on the departure of Auden and Isherwood for America in 1939.

———. *Enemies of Promise and Other Essays.* Garden City, N. Y.: Doubleday & Co. (Anchor Books), 1960. Contains the most extended comments on Isherwood's style.

———. "Introduction," *All the Conspirators.* London: Jonathan Cape, 1939. Favorable and illuminating comments on Isherwood's first novel.

DEMPSEY, DAVID. "Connolly, Orwell and Others: An English Miscellany," *The Antioch Review,* VII (March, 1947), 142–50. Discusses *The Memorial, The Berlin Stories,* and *Prater Violet.*

FORSTER, E. M. *Two Cheers for Democracy.* New York: Harcourt, Brace and Co., 1951. "The Ascent of F.6," pp. 263–65, offers an interesting contemporary reaction to the play. "English Prose Between 1918 and 1939," pp. 272–84, discusses Isherwood's attitude toward his readers.

FRASER, G. S. *The Modern Writer and His World.* New York: Criterion Books, n.d. Excellent short appreciation of Isherwood.

FRIEDMAN, NORMAN. "Point of View in Fiction: The Development of a Critical Concept," *PMLA,* LXX (December, 1955), 1160–84. Consideration of the camera eye as point of view.

GERSTENBERGER, DONNA. "Poetry and Politics: The Verse Drama of Auden and Isherwood," *Modern Drama,* V (September, 1962), 123–32. Comprehensive study of the plays.

GRANSDEN, K. W. *E. M. Forster.* New York: Grove Press, 1962. Contains a comparison of Isherwood with Forster.

HEARD, GERALD. *The Five Ages of Man.* New York: The Julian Press, 1963. Eccentric and fascinating work; sheds light on Isherwood's later novels.

KARL, FREDERICK R. *The Contemporary English Novel.* New York: Farrar,

Straus and Cudahy, 1962. Takes Isherwood at surface value, missing what is symbolic in his work.

KERMODE, FRANK. "The Interpretation of the Times," *Puzzles and Epiphanies.* London: Routledge & Kegan Paul, 1962. Pp. 121–30. Considers Isherwood and Anthony Powell.

LEHMANN, JOHN. *Autobiography:* I, *The Whispering Gallery.* New York: Harcourt, Brace and Co., 1955; II, *I Am My Brother.* New York: Reynal & Co., 1960; III, *The Ample Proposition.* London: Eyre & Spottiswoode, 1966. Important comments on (and letters from) Isherwood by one of his closest friends.

———. *New Writing in England.* New York: Critics Group Press, 1939. Study of the literature of the later 1930's in England, particularly Isherwood and his circle.

———. *New Writing in Europe.* Harmondsworth, Middlesex, England: Penguin Books, 1940. Repeats much of previous item.

LIDDELL, ROBERT. *A Treatise on the Novel.* London: Jonathan Cape, 1960. Compares Isherwood and Maugham.

POSS, STANLEY [recorder]. "A Conversation on Tape," *The London Magazine,* I, New Series (June, 1961), 41–58.

ROBERTS, Michael, ed. *New Country.* London: The Hogarth Press, 1933. A central anthology of 1930's writers; important introduction by the editor.

SPENDER, STEPHEN. "The Auden-Isherwood Collaboration," *The New Republic,* CXLI (November 23, 1959), 16–17. Protests the title *Two Great Plays* for Auden's and Isherwood's collaborations and maintains the authors would agree with him.

———. *World Within World.* London: Hamish Hamilton, 1951. Splendid autobiography with frequent and illuminating discussions of Isherwood.

SYMONS, JULIAN. *The Thirties.* London: The Cresset Press, 1960. Lucid, perceptive study of the period; emphasis on the Auden group.

WESTBY, SELMER and BROWN, CLAYTON M. *Christopher Isherwood: A Bibliography, 1923–1967.* Los Angeles: The California State College at Los Angeles Foundation, 1968. Largely comprehensive list of works by and on Isherwood.

WICKES, GEORGE. "An Interview with Christopher Isherwood," *Shenandoah,* XVI (Spring, 1965), 23–52.

WOOD, NEAL. *Communism and the British Intellectuals.* New York: Columbia University Press, 1959. Chapter IV offers a valuable contrast between the intellectuals of the 1920's and those of the 1930's.

WOOLF, VIRGINIA. "The Leaning Tower," *The Moment and Other Essays.* London: The Hogarth Press, 1952. Perceptive study of the Auden group from the perspective of Bloomsbury.

Reviews

AMIS, KINGSLEY. "A Bit Glassy," *The Spectator*, CCVIII (March 9, 1962), 309. *[Down There on a Visit]*.

Anon. "Naked, not Unashamed," *The Times Literary Supplement*, No. 3407 (June 15, 1967), p. 525. *[A Meeting by the River]*.

GRIGSON, GEOFFREY. *New Verse*, New Series, I (May, 1939), 54. *[Goodbye to Berlin]*.

GROSS, JOHN. "A Question of Upbringing," *The New York Review of Books*, VIII (May 18, 1967), 34–36. *[A Meeting by the River]*.

HAMPSHIRE, STUART. "Isherwood's Hell," *Encounter*, XIX (November, 1962), 86–88. *[Down There on a Visit]*.

HARDWICK, ELIZABETH. "Sex and the Single Man," *The New York Review of Books*, III (August 20, 1964), 4. *[A Single Man]*.

JEBB, JULIAN. *London Magazine*, II, New Series (April, 1962), 87–89. *[Down There on a Visit]*.

KAUFFMANN, STANLEY. "Death in Venice, Cal.," *The New Republic*, CLI (September 5, 1964), 23–25. *[A Single Man]*.

———. "Passages to India," *The New Republic*, CLVI (April 15, 1967), 22, 37–38. *[A Meeting by the River]*.

KAZIN, ALFRED. "Christopher Isherwood, Novelist," *The New York Times Book Review* (February 17, 1946), 1, 33. *[The Berlin Stories]*.

MAYNE, RICHARD. "Herr Issyvoo Changes Trains," *The New Statesman and Nation*, LXIII (March 9, 1962), 337–38. *[Down There on a Visit]*.

PRITCHETT, V. S. "Books in General," *The New Statesman and Nation*, XLIV (August 23, 1952), 213–14. *[The Memorial, Mr. Norris*, and *Goodbye to Berlin]*.

SPENDER, STEPHEN. "Isherwood's Heroes," *The New Republic*, CXLVI (April 16, 1962), 24–25. *[Down There on a Visit]*.

TRILLING, LIONEL. "The Wheel," *The Mid-Century* (July, 1962), 5–10. *[Down There on a Visit]*.

VIERTEL, BERTHOLD. "Christopher Isherwood and Dr. Friedrich Bergmann," *Theatre Arts*, XXX (May, 1946), 295–98. *[Prater Violet]*.

WAIN, JOHN. "Bergmann's Masterpiece," *The Spectator*, CXCII (June, 18, 1954), 742–43. *[The World in the Evening]*.

WHITEHEAD, JOHN. "Christophananda: Isherwood at Sixty," *The London Magazine*, V (July, 1965), 90–100. *[Ramakrishna and His Disciples]*.

WILSON, ANGUS. "The New and the Old Isherwood," *Encounter*, III (August, 1954), 62–68. *[The World in the Evening]*.

Index